ATTITUDE
IS EVERYTHING

A Tune-Up to Enhance Your Life

Second Edition

KEITH D. HARRELL

KENDALL/HUNT PUBLISHING COMPANY
4050 Westmark Drive Dubuque, Iowa 52002

Copyright © 1995, 1999 by Keith D. Harrell

ISBN 0-7872-5534-3

Library of Congress Catalogue Card Number: 98-67921

Printed in the United States of America.
10 9 8 7 6 5 4 3 2 1

DEDICATION

To Mom and Dad, whom I love so much. The early years truly made all the difference. You **both** inspired me and taught me to never give up.

To my sister, Toni. I will always be proud of your confidence and determination; you have always motivated me to do my best.

To my niece, Tania, my pride and joy. Greatness lives within you.

To my grandparents. Your love, your giving and your wisdom will always be remembered.

To my stepmother, Gretchen, all of my aunts, uncles and cousins. You all have given me so much more than I will ever be able to return. A special thanks to Uncle Lee "Mr. Positive," Aunt Blanche, Aunt Rose, Aunt Sue, Cousin Clayton, Jr. "Peanut," and to Cousin Bruce. Keep making a difference.

And most importantly to my God for giving me everything; life, knowledge, wisdom, and the ability to do His work.

Only the limits of our mindset can determine the boundaries of our future.

—Keith D. Harrell

CONTENTS

ACKNOWLEDGMENTS

Thanks to:

Pastor Creflo Dollar and Sister Taffi Dollar, World Changers Church International, College Park, Georgia, for sharing God's word with simplicity and understanding and a special thanks to Mother Dollar.

A person whose name and address I lost years ago. The book you mailed me helped change my life. Thanks to you and to the author of that book, Zig Ziglar. God bless you, Zig.

All my friends for planting a positive seed in me. Your friendship, support, and love are what has motivated me to go the distance.

Gelia Dolcimascolo, Dr. Marsha Gordon, and Carolyn Zatto for your editing, typing, and wonderful insights.

IBM and all the special IBMers I had the pleasure to meet and work with. And a special thanks to Diane Andrews and Craig Kairis, two of the greatest IBM managers a person could ever have worked for. Thanks for your love, hard work, and support. You helped make it possible.

Dr. Ed Metcalf, my friend, mentor, and vice president, who helped open the door to the IBM speaking world.

Dr. Myles Munroe for your encouraging words and your spiritual message. God will always be first.

Les Brown for helping me live my dream.

Tony Robbins for helping me rediscover my personal power.

Ivory Dorsey for your recommendations, support, and, most importantly, your friendship.

Hattie Hill for your wisdom, mentoring, and friendship.

William and Isabelle Gillis for sharing with me their positive attitude.

And a special thanks to Larry Winget, the person who really motivated me to write this book. Larry, your STUFF works. Thanks a million for all of your help and support. You motivated me to take action and took the time to show me how to get it done.

INTRODUCTION

The person who doesn't read
is no better off than the person who can't.
—*Author Unknown*

I once read on a poster in the Seattle University library that a person who reads one hour a day for a year will be known in his community in one year; if he reads one hour a day for three years, he will be known across the nation; and if he reads one hour a day for five years, he will be world-renowned.

By beginning to read this book, you already have made an investment in yourself—an investment that pays dividends when, and only when, you apply its principles and take action. The principle is that *attitude is everything*. A popular banner makes the point that "Attitude is a little thing that makes a big difference."

Because this is a different type of book, I want to provide you with a "user's guide" for it—a way to help you get the most out of the time you are about to invest in it.

This is not only a book to read; it is a book to do.

Since you've already picked it up and have read this far, you're undoubtedly interested in learning something about attitude and making positive changes of your own. As you work through the book, you'll learn about the power of attitude and how your attitude affects everything in your life. You'll learn that, no matter how old you are, what your position or station in life is, or what your gender or marital status is, your attitude will make a difference—and a positive attitude will make a positive difference.

Think about it. There are billions of people in the world, and one thing that every one of us has is attitude. The good news is, you don't have to buy it. The other news—not necessarily bad—is that if you want an attitude that works for you, that improves the quality of your life and enables you to accomplish your dreams, you have to work for it. You can't just sit around and wait for a positive attitude to happen to you.

Over the years, I've attended many seminars, read many books, listened to many tapes and interviewed many successful people on the subject of self-development—only to discover that nothing comes close to the power of a positive attitude. In fact, *the most valuable asset you possess is your attitude toward yourself and toward life.* As you will learn as you work through this book, what matters is not how much you know about maintaining a positive attitude, but how well and how consistently you put that knowledge to use.

How you use that knowledge is more vital than you may think. Recent studies link our thoughts—positive and negative—to our immune systems. Scientific research indicates that our minds and bodies act on each other in ways we had not foreseen. Positive attitudes seem to have a beneficial effect on our health and longevity.

Happily, many researchers believe—and I wholeheartedly agree with them—that positive attitudes are not a product of genetics and heredity but, with proper training, can be acquired.

The material you're about to read isn't simply cheerleading. If you want a positive attitude, you're going to need to be committed enough to work for it. This book is a guide toward developing the positive attitude that will work for you. It will provide you the information and the plan. However, it will be up to you to provide the effort and discipline to work the plan. Although it will take work, I promise you this—you'll get a wonderful return on your investment.

First, you'll look at the events that have influenced your life and at how you responded to those events. You'll determine whether your responses built a better attitude or were just more bricks in the wall you built between you and your success. Next, you'll consider a different facet of attitude and do tune-up exercises to make certain you are putting that facet of your attitude in order. Finally, you'll embark on a 21-day attitude tune-up that will help make a positive, effective, dynamic attitude a natural part of your life.

If something is simple or easy to do, most people are more inclined to do it. While what this book suggests is not exactly easy or simple, I have broken it into small bytes of information and small steps of action to make your goal easier to reach. It gives you little things that can change your thinking. By changing your thinking, you can change your beliefs. By changing your beliefs, you can change your actions. In fact, you can change your entire world and your future.

This book is written for people who are merely breathing but haven't yet started living. It is a guide to help you tune-up your attitude—but it will help you only as much as you are willing to help yourself.

Some chapters have a place for you to take notes. Some chapters ask you to think about and write down specific action steps. Take all the time you need, but do them. Remember, this is an investment in you. The light is green, so *go!*

I wish you a *super-fantastic*™ journey discovering the power of your attitude.

What Others Say

A positive attitude is the key to success for all
of us, and this book demonstrates countless ideas and suggestions
for tuning up our attitude! Keith has studied his topic well
and presents his information in a way that is easy to read and is
very enjoyable and helpful to all.

Les Brown
"The Motivator,"
Professional Speaker & Author

I'm impressed with the success you have had as a result
of your dedication.

Lou Holtz,
Head Football Coach,
University of Notre Dame

In business and in life generally, there is so much time wasted
on grousing, finger pointing, rationalizing and all those other
incredibly non-productive tendencies. If business people read
Keith's book and live by the principles and precepts which he so
clearly articulates, they will likely add years of productive actions
to their careers and, more importantly, to their pursuit of life.

E. Joseph McKay,
Senior Vice President, Mattel Toys

Each of us knows instinctively that attitude is important. Keith
brings this to life in a believable, enthusiastic and energizing way.

Kenneth R. Thornton,
General Manager, IBM North America

Your book *Attitude Is Everything*® hits the nail right on the head.
The longer we live, the more we will realize the impact our
attitude will have on our lives. Keith, your book will certainly
make the difference for many.

Lenny Wilkens,
Head Coach, Atlanta Hawks

This material provides an excellent vehicle for individuals to
focus on the importance of a positive attitude. You also do an
excellent job in terms of a "call to action," that is, to develop and
then actualize a game plan leading to continuous attitude
improvement. The questions, quotes and recommended readings
at the end of the chapters truly make this book a "user friendly"
document. In our changing world of health care these days,
material of this nature has become compelling reading.

Thank you for a significant contribution to the world of
positive attitude promotion.

Robert L. Shoptaw,
President and Chief Executive Officer,
Arkansas Blue Cross Blue Shield

Keith Harrell's *Attitude Is Everything: A Tune-Up to
Enhance Your Life,* is a must for anyone who desires to maximize
their potential and accomplish their dreams in life. This book
captures the foundational principles necessary to maintain
a right attitude in the midst of the distractions, challenges and
oppositions that confront all of us as we proceed towards our
goals. I highly recommend this book for the individual who
desires to move and remain on the cutting edge of success.

Dr. Myles Munroe,
Senior Pastor,
Bahamas Faith Ministries International

ABOUT THE AUTHOR

Keith Harrell has experienced success in the game of life. While growing up in Seattle, Washington, Keith aspired to become a professional athlete. He learned the art of competition on and off the basketball court. Today, he maintains that same winning edge in life because of one important journey—the desire to be the best! Almost two decades later, Keith is helping his clients to realize their personal best which affects their overall performance and outlook on life!

A nationally acclaimed speaker, trainer, and consultant, he is highly recognized for his innovative and enlightening presentations. He has many large corporate clients including IBM, Coca-Cola, Microsoft, and Marriott.

As a former IBM marketing executive, he traveled around the world positively impacting the professional and personal lives of customers, clients, and colleagues. His credentials include "BEST SPEAKER" by Guide Europe, InnsBruck, Austria, as well as "BEST SPEAKER" of several national and international conferences. His 13 years with IBM as one of their top training instructors prepared him professionally as a speaker, trainer, and consultant. Today, as president of Harrell Performance Systems, Inc. in Atlanta, Georgia, Keith's affiliation with the National Speakers Association and American Society for

Training & Development continues to expand his knowledge and effectiveness.

Keith has developed a series of presentations and seminars focusing on the importance of attitude, self-confidence, change, and teamwork. The "Attitude in Action" series highlights personal experiences and practical applications that enable his clients to maximize their professional and personal potential. He takes the "fix-it" or "kick-it" approach to developing an attitude of desired accomplishments.

1

ATTITUDE—WHAT IS IT?

When the race has started,
there is no sense looking back.

—*Keith D. Harrell*

From a personal perspective, as far back as I can re-member, I've heard about the importance of a positive attitude and the effect it would have in my life. I heard it at home, all throughout school, throughout Little League and college basketball, and throughout my days at IBM up to owning my own business.

Think back. How many times in your life have you heard about having a positive attitude? Although attitude is a powerful word that plays an important role in everyone's life, ironically many people don't know its meaning—or realize its impact on their lives. What, then, is attitude?

The *American Heritage Dictionary* defines the word *attitude* as "a state of mind or feeling with regard to some matter." Based on this definition, we all have an attitude because we all have feelings about something or someone.

For me, however, attitude has a one-word definition: *life.* Attitude is the difference-maker in life, a treasure that lies within you. A positive attitude is the key that jump-starts your life. Attitude dictates whether you're living life or life is living you. Attitude determines whether you are *on* the way or *in* the way.

Attitude also has an effect on people and situations around us. For example, I moved to Atlanta in 1989. When I first arrived, I bought tickets to an Atlanta Braves baseball game. When I asked the usher how to get to the upper-deck section indicated on my ticket, he said,

"Sit anywhere. The team can't win. Fans don't care. We all have bad attitudes. There won't be a big crowd, so sit anywhere." However, since I had a positive attitude, I sat right behind home plate and saw an outstanding game—Atlanta won.

In 1992, the Braves brought in a couple of veterans and a couple of outstanding rookies. During pre-season interviews, when asked what it was like to be playing for a losing team, the players all said roughly the same thing: "I've been a winner all my life. I'm bringing a whole new attitude to this team. As far as I'm concerned, we've got the nucleus, we have the talent to win it all."

Now, the hardest tickets to get in Atlanta are those to the Braves games. What really changed was the power of the team's attitude. You can't go anywhere in Atlanta today without bumping into an Atlanta baseball fan. Today, everybody in Atlanta wears Braves T-shirts and hats. Going to a Braves baseball game is a big event now, and it all started when a couple of players chose to be positive instead of negative.

Positive and negative—those are our attitude options. Each of us possesses both. Here comes the important part: Each of us chooses *which* will be our primary attitude.

Which is *your* attitude of choice: positive or negative? That's the first thing you need to find out. Here's an exercise that may help you determine which lens you're looking through:

1. After being laid off, you leap into action, making calls, sending out resumes. On your way to a promising job interview, your car's alternator gives out. You see this as an opportunity to devote time to self-searching and personal development and an excellent time to take up long-distance walking.

2. Three months ago, you landed a position with the company you wanted. You have your own office, a secretary, and a salary higher than you expected. Lately you sit looking out at the fabulous view from your office wondering why you're feeling left out . . . and you keep waiting for something negative to happen.

Since you're letting yourself see things from a negative perspective, you'll find something unpleasant in even the most superb circumstances, and vice-versa.

If you're a pessimist, expecting the worst, you'll never be disappointed—and that may even work to your benefit in some instances. If good fortune surprises a pessimist, though, will he really be able to feel the full excitement of the moment or be able to take full advantage of it?

Fortunately, according to Martin Seligman, a noted psychologist at the University of Pennsylvania, optimists—individuals with positive attitudes—are more successful than similarly talented pessimists. His research also in-

*A careful inventory
of all your past
experiences may disclose
the startling
fact that everything
has happened
for the best.*

—*Author Unknown*

dicates that negative attitudes can be changed to positive attitudes.

Each of us can decide to change our primary attitude—all we require is a little checking and testing. Most of us go to a physician or dentist once or twice a year to be aware of our health and to maintain our wellness. Most of us do the same for our cars; we take them to a quick-lube place every few thousand miles. Sadly, many of us don't give our mental well being that same type of attention.

When was the last time you had a "check-up from the neck up," as motivational speaker Zig Ziglar would say? When was the last time you had an "Attitude Tune-Up?"

Seligman's study has shown that our attitudes—positive or negative—affect whether we succeed or fail. *Executive Female* magazine quotes two studies that have shown that life insurance agents with optimistic attitudes sold more policies than did their pessimistic colleagues. Pessimists blamed failed sales attempts on themselves, which lowered their self-esteem and led to lower sales volumes. Optimists, rather than taking the rejections personally, had logical reasons prospects did not buy policies. Optimists not only sold 37% more than the pessimists did, they also remained on the job longer.

Furthermore, the last few years have produced mounting research that positive thinking aids in the healing process. British researchers have gathered evidence showing a tie between negative emotions and illness.

These studies are the tip of the iceberg when it comes to the power our minds have over our bodies. Positive thinking isn't just the assumption of a naive person—there are sound reasons for you to develop a consistently positive attitude.

Improving your attitude doesn't necessarily require making a 180-degree turn. Most of us are not 100% positive or negative all of the time. The most positive of us will feel a little down from time to time. The most negative of us are capable of experiencing or anticipating bright sunny days. Maybe all you really want is to learn to develop the skills that will help you pull yourself out of the dumps when you are down.

No one can dispute you can build a strong and powerful body through exercise, but it takes commitment and hard work. Studies now show you also have the power to build a positive attitude through mental exercises. However, that, too, takes commitment, hard work and ongoing effort. Are you ready to get started on your attitude? Let's kick it off by looking at four things you must learn to do:

> **1. Focus on handling stress.** The less stress you have, the more energy you'll have to exercise those positive-thinking muscles. While eliminating all stress from your life is unrealistic, you can add to your energy by concentrating on balancing your time. Look for ways to balance the time you spend at work with your leisure time. Some of us may need a larger percentage of our time devoted to work to

keep that balance. The right balance hinges on your individual needs—don't try to fit yourself into somebody else's mold. Leisure time for one person could be reading a book or watching TV; for another it might be fishing or taking a quiet walk. The only thing that matters is that you choose what makes **you** relaxed and happy.

Also, if you have specific challenges you're facing—whether it's being a caregiver to an elderly parent, being a single parent, or simply feeling lonely, seek out support groups, or join a hobby club (photography, hiking) or a fitness center. Look for a group with whom you can truly connect and with whom you'll feel accepted and recognized.

2. Identify your negative/pessimistic thoughts.
I'll never be able to finish this project; I'm not good enough to apply for this promotion. The moment you catch yourself thinking those pessimistic thoughts, counter them with facts: *Time is limited. I need help with copying and collating. Jeannie will help if I ask. If we get behind, I'll ask Mr. Jones if we can get more help. . . . They want five years of management experience and I only have three and a half. However, I have more computer knowledge and education than what they're asking. I'm going to give it a shot.*

Don't let up on defeating those negative thoughts. The more you fight them with facts and rational thinking, the more positive "muscle" you're building. You want this process to become automatic.

3. Tell a supportive person how you feel. Feelings left bottled up and unattended fester. You may also be isolating yourself, and many studies show that social isolation adds significant risk to your health.

If you want to apply for that position but can't shake those self-doubts, share them with a trusted friend. The support and encouragement you get will give you added ammunition against negative thinking.

4. Act to settle a problem. If you're stressed by a conflict with a co-worker, deal with the situation directly: "I know we disagree on how to implement this project; would you be willing to work it out with me?" Or, if a friend says or does something that hurts your feelings, tell him or her.

Resolving a problem will relieve your stress more quickly and effectively than just sitting back fretting and complaining about it. Even if you don't actually reach a solution, moving *toward* a solution is still less stressful than trying to ignore it.

These are common-sense strategies that will help you develop your positive attitude. They work because as you eliminate negative thinking you'll begin to enjoy a more positive feeling about yourself, which in turn will give you more energy for life.

■ ATTITUDE TUNE-UP #1

What is your personal definition of attitude?

■ ATTITUDE TUNE-UP #2

Describe your attitude toward:

Life—

Work—

Education—

Family—

Fun—

Higher Power—

Other People—

Review what you just wrote; take positive action on an element in your life that is less than positive . . . fix it or kick it. You only get one life.

■ ATTITUDE TUNE-UP #3

Each night, review the reactions you experienced to people and situations earlier that day:

A. What were your first thoughts?

B. Were they positive or negative?

C. If your thoughts were negative, did you immediately replace them with positive ones?

D. If they were positive, did you congratulate yourself?

■ ATTITUDE TUNE-UP #4

Describe the attitude you need to maintain or enhance your success in life.

▨ ATTITUDE TUNE-UP #5

What are some things you must do daily to reinforce this level of attitude?

QUOTES FOR YOUR ATTITUDE

Attitude is a treasure that
lies within you.

—Keith D. Harrell

Attitudes are contagious.
Are yours worth catching?

—Author Unknown

Attitude: You don't have to buy it,
but you do have to develop it.

—Keith D. Harrell

*R*ecommended *R*eading List

for

Chapter 1

See You Over the Top!
by Zig Ziglar

Success Through a Positive Mental Attitude
by Napoleon Hill and
W. Clement Stone

Attitude: Your Most Precious Possession
by Elwood N. Chapman

YOUR ATTITUDE REFLECTS
YOU

*One can only face in others what
one can face in oneself.*

—James Baldwin

*Fear cannot scare a
person who is
at peace with God.
There is no room,
opportunity, or place
for fear in such
a person.
When fear finds a home
in a person,
God is waiting to call.
Remember
you must have faith.*

—*Keith D. Harrell*

Although everyone has an attitude, not everyone has the same *type* of attitude. Some people's attitude toward life is an emphatic "YES." Others emulate the "Abominable No Man."

Some individuals' attitudes propel them along, helping them deal with challenges or overcoming obstacles and accomplishing their objectives. Others' attitudes are their anchors, slowing them down or stopping them altogether.

Think about how the people around you are described:

> "He's got a can-do attitude."
>
> "That George, he's always on top of things."
>
> "I don't know how Sarah does it; she can bring a smile to any situation."

Those are the "good guys"—the ones you like to be around and the ones you want to have on your team. Then there are the others:

> "You know Ellen. If there's not a problem, she can create one."
>
> "I know Hank is capable, but it's just too much work to get him to do anything."
>
> "I had lunch with Fred. To hear him tell it, nothing good ever happens to him."

You've met some of these individuals too. These are the ones who seem to carry a cloud above them.

You are successful when you remember that somewhere, sometime, someone gave you a gift. That gift is what started you in the right direction. Remember that you are blessed when you pass that gift on to help someone else.

—Keith D. Harrell

It's as though the world were divided into two kinds of people: Those who get up in the morning, throw open the window, take a deep breath and say, "Good morning, God!"; and those who drag themselves out of bed, stare out the window and say, "Good God . . . morning?"

You might be thinking, "That's fine for *your* life, but things are not going so well for me right now, and that's affected my attitude." If you're thinking that, you're among those who think attitude is a result of circumstance. When things go well, you have a good attitude, but when they don't go well, your attitude changes to match the circumstances. Because many people think that way, they are at the mercy of whatever happens to them.

George Bernard Shaw said, "People are always blaming their circumstances for what *they* are. The people who get on in this world are the people who get up and look for the circumstances they want and, if they can't find them, make them."

If you look around you, you can find dozens of examples of people whose attitudes don't fit their apparent circumstances. For example, one Sunday in church I heard a beautiful soprano voice behind me, so joyful that I had to turn around to see who it was. The voice belonged to a middle-aged lady sitting in a wheelchair. Her right arm was strapped to the arm of the chair and her left hand rested on a little platform touching the lever that controlled the chair. Someone had placed the hymnal in her lap. Evidently she had lost the use of all her limbs except the fingers of her left hand. Yet, there was a smile on her face, and she sang with obvious joy in her heart.

Mr. Shaw had the right idea. Life is full of circumstances—good or bad. The question is, do you use the circumstances as stepping stones toward your goals, or do you let the circumstances dictate your life?

Your attitude defines you; it affects the people around you and eventually it all comes back to you. That's true at home, at work, or in any other part of your life.

YOUR ATTITUDE AT WORK

Not long ago I was having lunch in a restaurant staffed with a fairly large number of "twenty-something" servers. The young man who waited on me was personable enough; he took my order after a reasonable period of time, but someone else caught my eye. The young woman serving the station next to mine was noticeably more energetic and she had a bigger smile and a warmer greeting. What impressed me most, however, was that when a party left one of her tables, she rushed over and cleared it while the other servers were standing around talking and waiting for the bus people to clean off the tables.

All of those employees were doing their jobs, but this young woman was doing more. I thought, "What a great attitude." She was making a difference. Her customers were happier because they were seated more quickly. Moreover, the two greeters were happier because they could move the customers more efficiently.

More importantly, this server was not only making a difference for those around her, she was also making a tangible difference for herself. She was clearing her own tables instead of waiting for someone else to do so, and she was able to get several extra customers (and their tips) during the shift.

Here's another example: Ever since I became a professional speaker and trainer, much of my work has been with corporations. Managers have invited me to speak to their sales forces, their office staffs, or their management groups. However, over the last several years, there has been a change in the tone of the invitations.

In my first year, the invitations were something like this: "Keith, we're going for a record year and I really want to keep my people pumped up. I'd like for you to help us raise our attitudes another notch."

During the next two years, the tone was not nearly as upbeat. The invitations were more like this: "Keith, we've got a real morale problem. Our people are more worried about their futures than their work. Frankly, I have to do something. Keith, I know you can help us and we're ready to get started. What can you do to help?"

In two short years, the workplace had changed dramatically. Companies were either "downsizing" or "rightsizing." Thousands of people who thought their lives were secure through retirement were suddenly vulnerable. Some became unemployed, and those who remained wondered when their turns would come. This was the kind of circumstance that can defeat you . . . if you let circumstance dictate your life. That's what happened to a lot of people. For others, the circumstance became an opportunity toward getting where they wanted to go.

Consider the following situation: Charley works in the computer industry. His story shows what somebody with a positive attitude can do when the circumstances look bleak. Here's how he tells it:

> I got fired from a job for having a bad attitude. My boss told me that I was doing pretty good work, but my negative attitude made it tough on him and everybody else in my department.
>
> I had a few weeks to think about it while I was looking for a job. My attitude had not helped me at all. I had done the work I was supposed to and I had done it as well as anybody else. But instead of being recognized for doing good work, I got fired for having a bad attitude. It was pretty obvious that I needed to change my attitude.
>
> In my next job, I promised myself that whatever happened, I would stay positive and do my job. I

wasn't going to let my attitude get in the way of my job security and advancement.

The second week I was there, they started downsizing. The only thing anybody talked about was who was going to be next. Maintaining a positive attitude was a little difficult. I sat down one night and wrote down the facts:

1. I have a job and, if I get fired, I'm no worse off than I was three weeks ago.

2. I'm learning some new skills, so I'm actually better off than I was three weeks ago.

3. If I work hard on my new skills, I'm going to be more valuable to this company or to some other company.

4. Sitting around stewing about it isn't going to help me, the company or anybody else.

After that, my plan was obvious. I spent several evenings a week working on my programming skills. Every day, I went to work with a smile and did my job as well as I could.

There was another round of downsizing, this time the president of the company was included. The new president came in and made a speech about cutting expenses and moving the company to California. That, of course, led to more rumors.

Before the move, I was offered a job with another company with a 20% increase in pay. My evening studying had paid off. The company I had worked for moved to California, but then they fired the president. I don't know what they're going to do now, but I have a much better job.

This time my attitude worked for me. With my old attitude I would have been among the first to go, and I wouldn't have had a clue what to do about it. With my new attitude, I knew I was able to deal with it. It helped me keep the job I had, and it helped me get a better one. I'm a believer.

Consider another situation: Lenny Wilkens, the coach of the Atlanta Hawks basketball team, is also a believer in having a positive attitude. As a player and as a coach, he had proved he could be a winner in the NBA (National Basketball Association). He is the winningest coach in NBA history, but many people wondered if he could continue winning with the Atlanta Hawks.

When Lenny arrived in Atlanta, he found a team that wasn't performing to his or the fans' expectations. Like other Hawks teams and years of Falcons football teams (and Braves baseball, until a few years ago), the Hawks carried a "Loserville" image.

It took only one season for everybody to see what Lenny Wilkens' Hawks would do. In Lenny's first season, the Atlanta Hawks experienced one of their best seasons. They won 57 games, which tied their franchise record. Their longest winning streak was 14 games. They even closed out the regular season by winning 6 out of their last 8 games.

That year, Lenny was voted NBA Coach of the Year. One day at lunch, I asked Lenny what made the difference. He told me there were a number of differences: He had traded for a couple of new players; he was a different type of coach from the previous one; but the most important factor was what the team *believed*. "I helped them change their beliefs," he said. "I helped them believe that they could win—that they had the talent to be a winning team. The big thing was attitude."

HOW ATTITUDE AFFECTS THE WORKPLACE

One of the challenges facing management and co-workers today is dealing with difficult people—people who have negative attitudes. It is important to note that a person with a negative attitude has the same power to influence others as a person with a positive attitude. The difference appears in the results. Positive attitudes in the workplace help improve communications and teamwork. Positive attitudes keep up morale and help increase productivity. The opposite can be said for negative attitudes. They dismantle teamwork, increase stress, and cripple productivity.

In the workplace, the big difference between the winners and the losers is often attitude. The salesperson who sells more, the manager who inspires her people, the manufacturing supervisor who sets the tone for everybody around him—all are good examples of what attitude does for you and everybody around you.

Remember that your real wealth can be measured not by what you have, not by where you are, but by the spirit that lives within you.

—Keith D. Harrell

How Attitude Affects Your Educational Experiences

If you have any doubts about the importance of attitude in education, ask a teacher or professor. I speak with students at many grade levels, and I speak to faculty groups, school administrators and school boards across the country. In every session, they give me new examples of why attitude is important.

A teacher will tell me that a part of his or her job is to help instill a positive attitude in the students, an attitude that keeps telling the students that they can win. I've asked how tough it is for the teacher or administrator to keep a positive attitude. There are problems handling discipline, absenteeism, parents, drugs, and in some schools, gangs and violence. In the face of all these obstacles, how can a teacher have a positive attitude, much less communicate one to the students? All teachers should recognize that within them is the power to remain focused and committed to knowing it's their gift and ability that can overcome all these obstacles and make the biggest impact on the lives of our youths.

How Attitude Works at Home

Some people seem to have the idea that since they have to be nice when they're out, they can be surly at home. Mom comes home from her job and says she's tired of smiling. Dad comes in and vents all the frustrations he has collected during the day. After all, if you can't be yourself at home, where *can* you be yourself?

I was raised in a home by parents that had their ups and downs. It wasn't always easy but my parents believed they could overcome their circumstances. They passed that attitude on to me. I don't remember ever wondering whether I would succeed or not. The only question was "What would I have to do to succeed?"

That's one of the most valuable gifts my parents gave me, along with wonderful examples of faith in God and teaching me to value others. Their teachings gave me a head start on my own attitude.

What can a positive attitude do in your home? Not only can it improve your own self-esteem, it can also help your spouse and children feel better about themselves. It can improve communication and solve little problems before they fester into big ones. It can help you express your love and care for your family members. Most importantly, it can make you much more pleasant to live with.

YOU choose. You can either concentrate on the negative circumstances: Your spouse doesn't understand you; the children aren't behaving according to your expectations; your lifestyle is not as rich or famous as you would like it to be. Or, you can concentrate on your attitude towards the circumstances and move on to where you want to be. What you will find is that when your attitude improves, the circumstances will improve.

Several years ago in Atlanta, Georgia, I learned a lesson from a Little League coach. He coached very young children, just a step up from t-ball.

> I learned in my first year that there is only so much I can do in terms of teaching those kids baseball. Our teams are selected by computer, so all of the teams in the league have some players with natural talents, some who may learn some skills and some who need to learn to play just for the fun of it.
>
> I work with them on their hitting and their fielding, and I try to get each of them to play to the best of their abilities. But, as far as I'm concerned, there's one thing that's more important than batting stance or fielding position. At the end of the season, I want all of those kids to feel good about themselves and what they've done. I want them to think of themselves as winners.

That coach dealt with attitude. For years he has coached winning teams. His attitude affects theirs. Their attitude makes them winners.

That's what attitude does. The rest of this book concentrates on how you can tune up your attitude so that you are not only a winner but also a force in helping others see themselves as winners.

◼ ATTITUDE TUNE-UP #1

In general, how does your attitude reflect you? Are you the "Good morning, God!" person more often than the "Good God . . . morning?" person?

What percentage of the time are you one or the other? Be as objective as you can.

◼ ATTITUDE TUNE-UP #2

Think of individuals in your life who affect you in a negative way. List them:

Think of individuals in your life who affect you in a positive way. List them:

◼ ATTITUDE TUNE-UP #3

When was the last time your attitude made a difference—bad or good—to those around you at work, at school, or at home?

As objectively as you can, think about and list the facts surrounding the situation and the personalities.

Reviewing the facts, would you or could you have done anything differently? How?

QUOTES FOR YOUR ATTITUDE

The best way to cheer yourself up
is to cheer everybody else up.

—Mark Twain

Believe that life is worth living
and your belief will help create the
fact.

—William James

Whether you think you can
or think you can't, you're right.

—Henry Ford

*R*ecommended eading List

for

Chapter 2

Puppies for Sale
by Dan Clark

First Things First
by Stephen R. Covey

Releasing Your Potential
by Myles Munroe, Ph.D.

3

ATTITUDES ARE
CONTAGIOUS

*He who does not hope to win has
already lost.*

—*Author Unknown*

One of the consequences of having a negative attitude is that you will always find other people to keep company with. You won't have trouble finding plenty of people who want to complain. Many individuals delight in finding something wrong about situations, things, or people. They have made a habit of being negative.

Next time you meet someone who is extremely negative, understand that his or her attitude affects you; it virtually rubs off on you. Negative thoughts, even other people's, have an impact on your emotions and your physical well being.

Of course, on the flip side of the same token, positive attitudes from friends, colleagues and even strangers also have an impact on you—a good one. For example, I discovered the impact of attitude on my life by looking back on situations in my past and then asking myself: What was the *event*? Who or what was *involved*? What was the *situation*? What *happened*? What *lessons* did I learn? Let me share some of the events that have affected my attitude and the important lessons I've learned.

> *Other people's actions can—and*
> *will—impact your attitude.*
>
> —*Keith D. Harrell*

No man has a chance to enjoy permanent success until he begins to look in a mirror for the real cause of all his mistakes.

—*Napoleon Hill*

Event

My dad dropped out of college.

Attitude Situation

My father dropped out of the University of Washington during his freshman year at the age of 19. He simply wasn't focused at school so he spent the following year working odd jobs as a construction worker. He soon became skilled as a wood-, wire-, and metal-lather. (Prefabricated construction components such as sheetrock have replaced the need for such skilled labor, but during the 1950s lathers built walls with lath and plaster.)

Attitude Change

Thirteen months later, my father "tuned-up" his attitude. He understood that initially he had not been motivated or disciplined enough to go to school. The year he spent working helped him to understand what he truly wanted for himself. My father set his goal to go back to school and graduate. He quit thinking about what he didn't like about school and concentrated on what he *did* like. By prioritizing what was really important and by resetting his goal, he was able to regain his focus.

My dad motivated himself by being his own coach. He learned that working hard and staying focused had helped him become successful as a construction worker, and he realized he would need the same hard work and focus to graduate from college and prepare himself for a different career path. Although he had dropped out of school, he did return to get his undergraduate degree in business education and his masters in education and administration; he recently retired after 32 years as a business accounting professor at Seattle Community College.

Attitude Lesson Learned

My father's experience was to have a profound and positive effect on me. Knowing that my dad had a tough time with school and yet had regained his focus taught me that although people can stumble and fall, they can pick themselves up.

As I was growing up, my dad often stressed the importance of an education. He preached: Never give up; stick with what you are doing, even when things get tough; stay focused; manage your time; and set goals for yourself. These guidelines stuck with me because I knew they were based on his personal experiences.

> *The people you allow to embrace*
> *your life ultimately have the greatest*
> *impact on your attitude.*
>
> —*Keith D. Harrell*

Event

At work, "negative" people were impacting my attitude: I was working for IBM in Atlanta as a training instructor. After thirteen years with Big Blue, I was suddenly informed by management that our company had split into several smaller companies and I was now reporting to one of these new companies. The date was June 10, 1992, and I will never forget that day for the rest of my life. I was told by my new management that I had only two options to choose from:

Option 1—Forget my *dream* and stop my outside activities as a motivational speaker.

Option 2—Quit.

Attitude Situation

I was frustrated and fearful. My love and passion for speaking had fulfilled a real need. When I tried to talk with some of my co-workers about my dream to be a professional speaker, I was disappointed. I was troubled by their negative comments toward my dream and what I wanted to do. They were bitter toward IBM, they were bitter toward life, and, consequently, they were bitter toward me. I realized one day that some people are like radioactive material—prolonged exposure causes damage. That's why I call such people "toxic," because even though their negative input and attitudes may

Congratulate yourself when you reach that degree of wisdom which prompts you to see less of the weaknesses of others and more of your own, for you will then be walking in the company of the really great.

—*Author Unknown*

not be felt right away, over time the exposure may be destructive.

Attitude Change

Rather than listen to the toxic people, I chose to contact four positive people I could rely on for good advice: my dad, my Aunt Rose, and my two good friends, Ralph Bianco and Calvin Saunders.

My dad said, "Son, someone may take your job, but don't ever let them take your dreams." He saw something positive in the situation. Aunt Rose's words were "With God as your partner, you will never fail." Ralph and Calvin echoed this attitude when they said, "Keep your faith. Don't ever forget you've got a special gift—go for your dream, and you know we are here if you need us."

Attitude Lesson Learned

Encouraged by their words, I felt special and believed I could make it in my own business. I knew I was going to give my future a 100%-plus effort.

I reconfirmed that, for me, God came first, my family and true friends would always be there for me, and all I had to do was ask.

> *When your attitude is positive, you are
> always prepared.*
>
> —*Keith D. Harrell*

Event

Reading *Think and Grow Rich: A Black Choice*, by Dennis Kimbro and Napoleon Hill.

Attitude Situation

After reading this book, I phoned Dennis Kimbro to introduce myself and thank him for writing it. I told him the book did more than simply inspire me; it taught me the principles that encompass the laws of success.

I'll never forget Mr. Kimbro's asking me what my purpose was. "I'm a motivational speaker," I responded quickly. "No, what is your *purpose*?" I began to stutter. I realized he was looking for a deeper purpose—my mission in life.

"Name ten of the last books you've read," Mr. Kimbro asked. I rambled off three or four and started stuttering again. He rattled off a list of books I should read that included *Law of Success* by Napoleon Hill and *The Wealth of Nations* by Adam Smith. The minute I hung up, I jumped in my car and drove to the nearest bookstore.

Attitude Change

I changed my thinking about what I was doing and took a deeper look at my mission, my purposes in wanting to be a speaker. I realized how much effort, research, and commitment my dream would take. My attitude changed from part-time positive to full-time positive. My behavior changed from just dreaming to *doing*.

In our phone conversation, Mr. Kimbro empowered me and, at the same time, coached me to think. He challenged both my knowledge and my purpose. He inspired me to take action. I took a "fix it or kick it" approach to my own attitude, which I chose to kick into a higher and deeper gear.

Attitude Lessons Learned

Knowledge is power, but only if the knowledge is being used. If I learn a new word from the dictionary each day, but never *use* the word in written or verbal form, the word I gathered is useless.

"Power comes from knowing how to do something. People with power are people who know how to get things done, and sometimes knowing how to do something is virtually the same as having done it. So when we educate ourselves, we build power to accomplish our goals." That's a great quote from Wynn Davis' *The Best of Success*.

I also discovered the importance of having a purpose in life and not waiting until tomorrow to do what I could today. Having a purpose in your life keeps you on track.

Every failure and success will teach you a lesson that you need to learn if you will keep your eyes and ears open and be willing to remain humble.

—*Keith D. Harrell*

Purpose is the fuel that feeds success.

—*Keith D. Harrell*

Don't be intimidated by the concept of "purpose." It doesn't have to mean something as targeted as saving the rain forest, or writing the proverbial "great American novel," or finding a cure for cancer. Your purpose can be a simple personal philosophy, such as treating everyone with respect, kindness and compassion, or meeting life with your mind and heart open. These kinds of purposes require just as much work and goal setting as those more oriented to conventional success.

Many of my professional speaking colleagues entered the field because they wanted to make a difference in people's lives. It's a personally fulfilling purpose and brings success on many levels.

Some of us may have the same purpose throughout our lives. Others of us will change our purpose as we learn, grow, and change. The point is to establish a mission for yourself and keep checking it: Is what I did today supporting and advancing my mission or purpose? If the answer is "no," think about how you will change your behavior for tomorrow.

I learned that, by controlling my thoughts, I can control my attitude. "The greatest potential for control tends to exist at the point where action takes place." This statement by Louis A. Allen is one of my favorites.

When we control our decisions, we control our actions; a positive attitude helps produce a positive action. Here's an example:

> Through a friend of a friend, and at a rather steep price, I got tickets—fourth row center—to an NBA playoff basketball game. A man approached and loomed over me saying, "Haul it out of here, pal; these are my seats!" My first reaction was to yell back, "Take a hike!" Instead I stopped to think: "No way I am giving up these seats. But if it gets ugly, we could both be thrown out of the arena." So, with a concerned look on my face I said, "Maybe I read my tickets wrong." I pulled out my tickets and placed them next to his so we could compare. His tickets were for seats 6 and 8, row 4, Section 101— the section directly opposite mine. "Well, I do have your seat numbers all right, but you're in section 101 on the other side of the court. Looks like we both have the best seats in the house." The man, relieved, smiled, mumbled an apology and happily rushed off to the right section.

The experience could have been a complete disaster if I had followed my initial thoughts. By choosing to control my thoughts and maintaining a positive attitude, we all enjoyed a great basketball game.

Whether someone approaches you in a negative, combative manner, or whether you need to make the first move in a situation, the ball is in your court. If you set a positive tone, the chances of a positive outcome are very good.

I realized that, by controlling my attitude and my thoughts, I controlled my own destiny. There's a lot of controlling going on in all our professional and personal lives. Someone or something always has a certain amount of control over us. Every day we meet individuals who need to control those around them; sometimes *we* have that same need. Fortunately, each of us has the ability to control ourselves. How we choose to use that control can alter our life's direction for the bad or the good.

I had no control over the attitude of friends and co-workers who thought my dreams and goals were inaccessible, if not outright fantasies. I chose not to be influenced by negative attitudes, but to keep my attitude positive. When I started my own speaking, training and consulting business, Harrell and Associates, Inc., I took control of my destiny. I knew that I had unlimited potential and that my business would succeed. My plans were not based on fanciful fiction—I was prepared to give it total effort and dedication. From past experience, I knew that maintaining a positive attitude would give me limitless energy and commitment to keep that dream alive and growing.

Finally, I learned to give thanks to people, no matter who they were or what they did—to let them know when they made a difference. We all say "thanks" and "thank you," but it can sound and feel a little hollow if we do it by rote.

Be specific when you thank someone. "Thanks for being willing to stay late to help me finish the project. Your support and positive attitude gave me more energy and spurred my creativity." When we get a thank you like that, we truly feel appreciated.

Don't ever underestimate the power of "thank you" in your life and the lives of those to whom you give your thanks.

> *Patience, persistence, and a positive attitude will always produce results.*
>
> —*Keith D. Harrell*

Event

Meeting Les Brown, a highly acclaimed speaker who speaks to Fortune 500 companies and conducts personal and professional seminars around the country.

Attitude Situation

It took effort to meet Les Brown; his time is in great demand and I was determined to speak with him. Since I was just starting my speaking career, I thought it would be a good idea to talk to a proven professional.

After several months of my calling Les' office, someone called me back to inform me that Les would be speaking at a hotel in Atlanta the next weekend. I thought this would be my chance—my opportunity to meet him. I was so excited I got up at 5 A.M. that day, even though I knew his seminar didn't start until 11.

Les made a strong impression on me and a positive impact on my attitude. As I listened to him speak, I kept thinking about the tremendous talents he possessed. He was dynamic, he had a great sense of humor and an infectious laugh, and he told the most outstanding stories of overcoming personal adversity.

As I was driving home, I felt both motivated yet discouraged. I was motivated because I had just heard one of the best public speakers in the business, and I had established a connection with this person who said he would review my videotape and give me feedback. I was discouraged because I still kept questioning my own abilities and second-guessing myself and my dream to become as great a speaker as Les.

A month later, Les called me at about 11:30 one night, after having reviewed my videotape. "Keith, the quality of this tape is so bad, I can hear you but I can't *see* you. We need to work on getting you a better quality tape—but you have real potential. Don't ever forget that," he said.

For every victory and loss there is a lesson in disguise. Without life's ups and downs and temporary joys and defeats, you would never know the stock of which you are made.

—Keith D. Harrell

Attitude Change

I changed my attitude by reminding myself to remain humble and to realize that we all are blessed with our own unique gifts.

Attitude Lessons Learned

I learned that we must be prepared to accept other people's feedback and grow from their criticism, and that it can be most important to have a mentor or coach who gives advice and direction, especially if that person is directly connected to your chosen profession. His having reviewed the tape and having given me the feedback he'd promised emphasized a simple but important lesson: *Be a person of your word. When you make a commitment, follow through. If you tell someone you are going to do something, do it.*

Finally, I learned how the magic and positive attitude of one individual can keep another person from quitting.

Looking back on all of the unsuccessful phone calls I made in my attempt to talk to Les Brown, I realize it was his receptionist, Sue Burkhart, who kept giving me hope—and the desire to keep trying. She was one of the most courteous people I had ever had the pleasure of speaking with. Every time we spoke, she was always upbeat and positive. I remember calling one day from the Chicago airport.

"Hello, Sue, is the main man in today on this late Friday afternoon?"

"Is this my favorite person, is this Mr. Attitude? I know by that positive upbeat voice it must be you, Keith."

"Sue, you sure know how to make a person feel special. Is Mr. Brown in?"

"No, sorry, Keith, he is on the road again."

"Sue, did you give him my last ten messages? You know he hasn't called me back yet."

"Keith, you stay positive, honey, and keep calling. I know one day your persistence is going to pay off."

"Sue, you bet I am."

"Don't ever forget, Keith, you've got something special."

"Boy, Sue, you are just like Les with those positive words of encouragement."

"I'll keep trying, you know I will."

Sue's attitude and professionalism were *super-fantastic™*.

When is the last time you looked at your job, your family, your relationships, or life itself to analyze how they are affecting you and your attitude? When was your last attitude tune-up? Last week, last month, last year? It's time for you to take action *now*! Tune-up the one thing that affects everything you do and how well you do it: Tune-up your attitude and *enhance your life*.

▣ ATTITUDE TUNE-UP #1

Answer the following questions briefly:

1. Are you focused? If not, why not?

   _____

2. Are you managing your time properly? If not, why not?

   _____

3. What are your goals?

   _____

4. Are they written down? If not, why not?

   _____

5. What additional education/training do you need to achieve the success you want?

   _____

6. What are you doing to enhance your current skills, and what are you doing to learn new skills?

_____

7. What personal development course are you going to invest in?

_____

■ ATTITUDE TUNE-UP #2

Reflect on the types of people you associate with. Develop a list of family members and friends who support and encourage you.

Remember, there is nothing that compares to helping another person in need.

Start by being a friend to yourself. This is important because, to have a friend, you must be a friend. Be a friend by helping someone. Put yourself in the circle of "what goes around comes around." If you want to add to your support system, get involved in community groups, professional and charitable organizations, church activities, alumni associations, and so on. When you encourage others, you are in turn encouraging yourself.

■ ATTITUDE TUNE-UP #3

What criticism have you heard that you need to transform into positive directions to enhance your personal growth?

Make a list of or think about the people who care about you enough to give you honest feedback.

_____	_____
_____	_____
_____	_____

Whom can you choose to become your mentor or coach? To enhance your performance? What is that person doing that you are not?

Seek out the people in your field you need to meet, and then contact them.

Without analyzing and modifying your attitude, how can you enhance your performance? Take a few minutes at the beginning or end of your day to take the first steps in tuning up your attitude. Start by identifying the event, focusing on the situation, and discovering your lesson learned.

Event:

Attitude Situation:

Attitude Change:

Attitude Lesson Learned:

■ ATTITUDE TUNE-UP #4

Take time to identify your purpose. Use that understanding to take control of your thoughts. Who would you like to give thanks to for making a difference in your life? Do it *now*.

QUOTES FOR YOUR ATTITUDE

We have only to move confidently in the
direction of our dreams and live the life
we have imagined to meet with a success
unexpected in common hours.

—Henry Thoreau

How we think shows through in how
we act. Attitudes are mirrors of the
mind. They reflect thinking.

—David Joseph Schwartz

The important thing to remember is that if
you don't have that inspired enthusiasm
that is contagious—whatever you do have
is also contagious.

—Danny Cox

*R*ecommended eading List

for

Chapter 3

The Best of Success
by Wynn Davis

Law of Success
by Napoleon Hill

The Wealth of Nations
by Adam Smith

Are *You* Destroying Your Attitude?

The loudest voice we hear is our own, so listen closely.

—Keith D. Harrell

Are you destroying your attitude with your own internal conversation? Are you limiting your performance because of negative self-talk? You may be asking, What is self-talk? How can it limit me if it's just my internal voice talking to myself? If it's that important, how can you change negative self-talk to positive self-talk? The following story will show you how I learned some answers to those questions:

> The year was 1960. I was five years old, tall and skinny, and it was my first day of kindergarten. I was psyched! My mom had my school clothes laid out—shirt, socks, shoes and two pairs of trousers from which to choose. I liked both pairs of pants so much I put them both on! After Mom and I sorted out the trouser situation, I gobbled down breakfast and ran to the car, jumping into the back seat. "It's just you and me today," my mother said. "Sit up front next to me. I am so proud of my little man— it's your first day of school."
>
> "Mom, isn't that my school? Is it the tallest building in the world?" I asked as we approached the school.
>
> Excited about my enthusiasm, she replied, "Yes, son, as far as Mom's concerned, it *is* the tallest building in the world today."
>
> I was so excited that, as I walked into the classroom, I said hello to the first group of kids I saw. Most of them seemed to be just as excited as I was.
>
> When class started, the teacher, Miss Peterson (her name remains in my memory even after all this time),

announced that she wanted all the students to stand and introduce themselves as she called out their names. She wanted them to express their feelings about their first day of school.

My moment of truth came when Miss Peterson called my name first. I jumped up and tried to speak, but all I could get out was, "My, my, my, my, my, my-y-y- . . ."

A little girl in pigtails in the back of the room yelled, "He can't talk—he stutters!"

"You're too tall—you shouldn't be in our room," a little boy added. I guess I had stuttered at home before, but I had never met with such stinging response. Also, I had never realized I was "too tall." I was embarrassed and mortified.

As I look back, however, I realize the loudest voice I had heard was my own: "You can't talk. You just stutter. You're too tall. You shouldn't even be in the class. I didn't think school would be like this." Finally, when they let us out for recess, I ran home—the fastest I've ever run in my life.

As I ran up on the porch, Mom was there, ready to give me a loving hug, as only a mother can. "I just hung up the phone with Miss Peterson," she said, "and I know what happened. I am proud of you. My little man tried, and even though you are not able to say your name as well as you would like, that's okay. This is going to be a challenge, but I'm convinced that if we work hard, one day—and I do mean one day—all the kids will listen when you say your name loud and clear." She ended this pep talk with one strong, simple phrase. "Son, don't ever forget that you are special." Bolstered by her love and understanding, I returned to school the next day.

I learned an important lesson that day—a big lesson for a little boy in kindergarten. Today, I understand it was my mother's positive words that replaced my negative thoughts and self-doubts.

For the next six years I worked with a speech therapist. From then on, however, when the kids at school teased me about stuttering and not being able to speak clearly, I would just think about all the positive input I had received from my speech therapist, from my teacher and, most importantly, from my mother.

Our attitudes and beliefs are influenced so much by what people say. As I look back on that first day of school, I realize I could have become programmed to be positive or negative right then. Like computers, our minds can be programmed. Yet the most advanced computer in the world is only as productive as the program it's running.

We are all faced with challenges every day—in business, in education, in sports, in simply handling everyday pressures. Hundreds of different situations program our attitudes each day, and most of these have the potential to be both positive and negative. The subconscious mind

I am thankful for the adversities which have crossed my pathway, for they have taught me tolerance, sympathy, self-control, perseverance and some other virtues I might never have known.

—*Author Unknown*

never sleeps. You can't pull a fast one on the subconscious. Whatever it has heard—from others and especially from our own self-talk—it records . . . and keeps.

In other words, most people are allowing their brains to be programmed indiscriminately. The computer adage, garbage in, garbage out, as it applies to our own very personal computer—the brain—should be stated as garbage in, garbage stays. The brain hears negative things and accepts them as truth. Many of us have behavior patterns today that were programmed into our brains at a very tender age. The information that was recorded by our brain could have been completely inaccurate or even cruel.

Think of a sunflower seed you plant and nurture. That seed was programmed by nature to be a sunflower. Don't even think about trying to make it into a pumpkin or a rose. It was programmed to be a sunflower and that's the end of it. Some of us were programmed at a very early age to behave a certain way. Maybe part of your programming tells you that you're not very smart and you believe it and your actions bear it out. You might have a learning disorder, but maybe you simply have faulty programming. After all, there are many people with serious learning disorders who were programmed by loving parents and caring teachers to believe they could overcome their barriers . . . and they did.

Maybe it's time to plant new seeds.

WHAT IS POSITIVE SELF-TALK?

I define positive self-talk as "a way to override our past negative programming by erasing or replacing it with a conscious, positive internal voice which helps us face new directions."

Self-talk—that incessant little voice we listen to all day long—acts like a seed in that it programs our brains and affects our behavior. Fortunately, the information in our brains can be reprogrammed. We have the choice to take a closer look at what we're saying to ourselves and start reprogramming for personal and professional success.

Consider three of the most common influences that can program us daily and that have the potential to have positive or negative impacts on our attitude and self-talk:

1. **Television:** With all the violence on television today, it's no wonder crime and violence in some areas of the country are higher than ever before. However, on the positive side of television are educational, spiritual, sports, comedy programs, and even sitcoms focusing more on the importance of positive values. Start monitoring what you watch on television.

   Furthermore, studies show that the subconscious mind is the most receptive five minutes before we doze off at night. This period is when the mind also reviews events, experiences, and thoughts that occurred to us that day. Typically, we review the negative stories. We also might watch the late news as we doze off. Talk about negative influences: Murders, wars, family violence, baseball strikes. No wonder we wake up in an agitated state of mind some mornings.

2. **Newspapers:** Many people program themselves every morning or every evening by reading their newspaper, which contain both positive and negative articles. Make a habit of finishing your paper by finding a positive story to program your attitude and your self-talk.

3. **Other people:** What other people say and do greatly influences us and impacts our self-talk. Pay close attention to what people say and do, and filter out the negative comments or actions.

What type of programming have you been running your life with? Start now by using your self-talk to reprogram all past negative programming.

WHAT ARE THE BENEFITS OF POSITIVE SELF-TALK?

Self-talk empowers you with the capability to control your destiny through the most accessible tool at your disposal: Controlling what you say to yourself. This theory may sound too simple and too good to be true.

It is simple, but the truth is, changing old habits and patterns is difficult. You must be committed and determined to keep your self-talk positive. You need to monitor your self-talk every waking moment of the day. However, don't expect to be perfect 100% of the time. Some of that faulty self-talk you're spouting is rooted in decades of negative programming. Stay committed and determined, but be patient and kind to yourself. Otherwise, you'll be adding more negative thoughts to your self-talk.

The benefits of altering your self-talk are unlimited. If you're willing to work at it, you can get what you want.

If you are a young person going to school, use positive self-talk to:

> Stay in school and learn as much as you can
> Cope with and override peer pressure
> Stay away from guns and drugs

If you are a parent, use positive self-talk to:

> Be a patient, understanding person who listens to and treats your family with respect
> Be a positive role model for your family
> Encourage yourself to spend quality time with your family
> Cope with and overcome stress and the challenges of life

If you believe in a Higher Power, use positive self-talk to:

Keep an open heart and mind

Pray and worship

Motivate yourself to spread the word of your faith

Overlook the wrongs of others

If you are a teacher or professor or trainer, use positive self-talk to:

Treat peers and students with respect

Reinforce your commitment to teaching

Encourage yourself to embrace change

Educate, motivate and inspire your students

If you are in a bad relationship, use positive self-talk to:

Seek professional advice or counseling

Communicate better with others and move forward without looking back

Enhance your self-esteem during these difficult times

If you are employed, use positive self-talk to:

Handle any increase in workload and be a team player

Every failure is a blessing in disguise, provided it teaches some needed lesson one could not have learned without it. Most so-called failures are only temporary defeats.

—*Author Unknown*

Empower you to accept change

Accept new responsibilities

If you are unemployed, use positive self-talk to:

Keep your confidence high while you seek a new
job

Learn a new skill or trade

Stay positive

If you are an athlete, use positive self-talk to:

Set your performance goals

Overcome defeat and bounce back

Motivate you to outdo yesterday's performance

If you are a salesperson, use positive self-talk to:

Enhance your confidence in your selling skills

Overcome not making quotas

Improve customer relationships

If you are a homemaker upset at being homebound with young ones, use positive self-talk to:

Reinforce the great job you are doing for your
family's success

Remind you that it takes a special person to do what you do

Help you realize that your role *is* a job—and the most valuable one in the world

Accept that your role was—and is—your choice

Below are examples of negative self-talk I have overheard. As you read them, compare them to your own conversations and add your own phrases to the list.

EXAMPLES OF NEGATIVE SELF-TALK

I just know it won't work.

I hate my job and the people I work with.

I am not artistic.

I am too old to do anything else in life.

I just don't have the energy to make a change.

I ought to take care of it now, but it'll wait until tomorrow.

Nothing ever seems to go right for me.

I will start my diet tomorrow.

I am just no good at anything.

If it weren't for bad luck, I wouldn't have any luck at all.

I am at the end of my rope.

If only I were smarter.

Mondays are not good days for me.

EXAMPLES OF POSITIVE SELF-TALK

I know it will work, because I will put all of my
effort into making this a success.

With all the people out of work today, I am lucky
to have a job.

I am creative in my own way.

Age is only a number, and the number I carry
today is Number One.

I have been storing my energy and I am now
ready to handle change.

Tomorrow is not guaranteed. I won't put off until
tomorrow what I can do today.

Today I will be judged by my effort and my
positive attitude, which will ensure that every
day is a *super-fantastic*™ day.

I feel better about myself today because I know
the importance of a healthy diet.

I'd make a lousy anybody else, but I can be the
best *me* in the world.

I don't live my life on luck. I live my life by
having faith, persistence, and a positive
attitude.

Today is the first day of the rest of my life. I am
enhancing my skills daily.

I can't get to Friday until I step on Monday—and
every day is an opportunity.

ATTITUDE TUNE-UP #1

Start listening to your voice. Every day, write down your self-talk, both positive and negative. This exercise will help you gain control over the words that affect your attitude.

Negative Self-Talk

Positive Self-Talk

▊ ATTITUDE TUNE-UP #2

Three Steps to Changing Negative Self-Talk

Step l: Reverse all negative input and self-talk and turn those comments into positive directives. Tell your negative inner voice to be silent and then restate the phrase in a positive, present or future tense.

> Example—Change "I can't pass this class; it's too hard" to: "I am going to pass this class. I will get a tutor, and I will study. I will pass."

Step 2: Adopt positive self-talk phrases and repeat them daily. Write them down and put them in conspicuous places as reminders, or record them on a cassette with or without your favorite music. Play the recordings regularly each day.

Step 3: Take the three-minute mirror test: Look directly into a mirror and state positive self-talk phrases out loud. By doing so, you are then confirming to yourself that you accept these positive inputs and that you are in control of your life. If you have difficulty with the mirror test, ask yourself what negative programming you have experienced over the years to cause you to avoid this step.

Quotes for Your Attitude

You are what you think you are
all day long.

—Ralph Waldo Emerson

You are today where your thoughts
have brought you.
You will be tomorrow where your
thoughts take you.

—James Allen

If you can imagine it,
you can achieve it.
If you can dream it,
you can become it.

—Keith D. Harrell

*R*ecommended eading List

for

Chapter 4

What to Say When You Talk to Yourself

by Shad Helmsetter, Ph.D.

Chicken Soup for the Soul

by Mark Victor Hansen and Jack Canfield

You Can't Afford the Luxury of a Negative Thought

by Peter McWilliams

5

COACHING
THE POWER WITHIN

*Affirmation—seeking to confirm
a positive belief.*

—Keith D. Harrell

An affirmation is a positive statement of truth. To affirm is to make firm in your mind. It is stating something to be true regardless of all evidence to the contrary. It is a type of mental activity used for building consciousness or awareness. It lifts you out of false thinking. An affirmation contains the elements of your belief, attitude, and motivation.

In my opinion, this statement clearly defines the meaning of affirmations and how to use them effectively.

An affirmation is made up of words—words charged with power, conviction, and faith. Every time you speak, atoms of your body are affected; their rate of vibration is either raised or lowered. The purpose of an affirmation is to impress the subconscious mind, for what is **im**pressed is **ex**pressed. This process involves *repetition, feeling,* and *imagining.*

Repetition is very important. By *repeating* the affirmation, you send a positive response to your subconscious, which, as we discussed in Chapter 2, accepts whatever you tell it. When done properly, this triggers positive *feelings* that, in turn, drive action. *Imagining* is the process that allows you to see the affirmation in your mind; once you can see it in your mind, you'll be closer to achieving it in your life.

Affirmations, repeated several times each day, every day, serve to reprogram your subconscious with positive thinking. Remember, too, that as positive thinking takes

*Anyone can "start,"
but only the thoroughbred
will "finish"!*

—*Keith D. Harrell*

hold in your mind, your body responds accordingly. If you're having trouble accepting this concept, which has considerable scientific evidence and research confirming it, think about this somewhat ordinary occurrence: blushing. Many of us blush when embarrassed. Sometimes it might be because of something we hear or see. We haven't actually exerted ourselves to the point that blood rushes to our faces causing them to redden; it's the mere thought or sight of a situation that triggers this physiological reaction. If we have this kind of physical display from a thought, why is it so difficult to believe that a positive thought could affect our bodies in a beneficial way? Research also shows that the simple act of smiling causes your brain to release a stream of chemicals that makes you feel good. The best things in life really are free. SMILE!

Affirmations not only help to keep you positive, they also stir the power within you. This power within you needs to be coached and guided to maximize your performance. No one can motivate you but *yourself*—motivation comes from the inside out. Thus, we each need to use our own internal coach to guide the power within us. Your attitude coach is a coach who lives within you, always seeking to affirm a positive action or event.

Championship teams and successful people share several elements: the joy of success and achievement, hard work, dedication, desire and commitment, and good coaching and direction. As naturally talented as Michael Jordan is in basketball, or Oprah Winfrey is as a TV personality or Zig Ziglar is as a motivational speaker, each has needed a coach and each has needed direction.

Athletes also devote a significant portion of each day to physical training and practicing their sports. However, most athletes, amateur or professional, are devoting more and more time to *mental* training. Pole-vaulters see themselves through every step of their jump. They not only visualize their goals, they also imagine exactly what their bodies feel like when they make perfect vaults. Research shows we learn faster with this type of mental visualization. Sports psychologists say that such mental training sends neuromuscular signals that give the athlete a stronger, more effective performance during the actual event or game.

Athletes—and successful individuals in any field—used affirmations long before the concept of positive programming became popular. Instinctively, they knew to keep telling themselves to win, to see and feel themselves give a winning performance; to listen as much to their internal attitude coaches as to their living, breathing coaches.

Think of your attitude coach as a voice inside you that predicts the outcome in advance and, by doing so, it gives you the personal power to endure. Your attitude coach will guide you to a winning season, much like the Super Bowl in football, or the World Series in baseball. Your new attitude coach *can and will* direct you to winning the biggest game of all, *the game of life*.

It doesn't matter whether you are self-employed or work for a Fortune 500 company, or what field you are in. It doesn't matter whether you are in school or out of school, unemployed or the president of a successful company. There is not a person living who at some time doesn't need support, encouragement, a pep talk, direction, or a plan of attack. Think of all the situations you know in which someone, by having a strong belief, a conviction, a direction, a positive action or affirmations, successfully accomplished their goal.

I use affirmations in my own life to achieve rewarding results. For example, during my senior year at Garfield High School in Seattle, Washington, our basketball team was two games away from winning the state championship. We were favored to win it all. Going to the state tournament, we were undefeated—22-0.

On the day of the semifinal game, the *Seattle Times* printed a story saying we were one of the best teams ever in Washington's history. The game started very slowly; nothing seemed to be working. The Lincoln High School team from Tacoma seemed to have scouted us well. They broke our press, played good defense, and shot the ball extremely well. We found ourselves trailing throughout the entire game. With about three minutes left and our team down by six points, our coach called a time-out. As I walked to the bench, I detected a sense of defeat in my teammates. During the time-out, there were only negative comments from them complaining about what *hadn't* happened. I stood up,

Think well before you speak because your words may plant the seed of either success or failure in the mind of some other person.

—*Adopted from poster entitled "Words of Wisdom"*

looked directly at my coach, and said, "We are going to win this game. Give me the ball."

I didn't realize it then, but that statement was a powerful affirmation. That affirmation did something for everyone, because we came out of that time-out and won the game by seven points. The power of my belief empowered me, and my actions in turn empowered my teammates.

People often use positive words to empower themselves and other people. Affirmations are especially needed when life deals us major blows.

> I met Carol Hughes and her son, Jonathan, in Atlanta, Georgia after one of my seminars. She shared with me the fact that Jonathan, born three months prematurely had cerebral palsy. At first, Carol was devastated, and spent the next year very depressed. Then she began to seek answers and guidance. "I was determined to change my own attitude," she says. "As a result of my change in attitude, Jonathan and I are two of the happiest people I know." Jonathan is now 18, "and we always find a way for him to do whatever he wants, because we know anything is possible with the right attitude."

CREATING YOUR OWN AFFIRMATIONS

The statements you design for your affirmations must be positive and in the present or future tense. Do not use words such as "try," "wish," or "hope." These words have no place in your affirmations. Your statement is affirming and confirming that what you want to become the truth is already the truth—a done deal. Do not say, "I'll try to learn," or "I hope I can be a better person," etc. Instead, declare, "I am learning all the material presented to me in class," or "Each day I am a better, stronger, more balanced person."

You want to affirm what is realistic; steer clear of fantasies. I am a positive thinker, but if one of my affirmations were, "I am the Founder of Mrs. Fields' Cookies and I own cookie stores all over the world," I would be in for a fall. First of all, Mrs. Fields is the founder of the company, Mrs. Fields' Cookies. It's also highly unlikely I'll ever go into the cookie business.

Reach beyond your current comfort zone with your affirmations. Keep your affirmations a step or two beyond where you're presently walking, but don't cancel out your affirmations by stating something that may be a remote possibility.

Start using affirmations to coach *you* and your team to victory in all of life's efforts. Do it *now*!

YOUR AFFIRMATIONS

List some affirmations you can use to ignite the power within you. Repeat these affirmations over and over as often as possible. Say them to yourself with conviction and authority, believing every word you say, and see them take shape and become your reality. Repeat them until they become part of you.

Affirmation Tune-Ups

What is the first thing you do when you wake up? Many people complain. They complain about what time it is or about their lack of sleep. They complain about not going to bed early. Do you set your alarm clock to go off at a certain time, only to hit the "snooze" button or become annoyed at the clock when the clock is only doing its job? Such negative reactions impact negatively on your attitude. Change the way you get up—it will make a difference. For example, this first step is designed to jump-start your day by giving *positive* recognition as soon as your eyes open.

■ Attitude Tune-Up #1

After waking up, look into a mirror and read this 30-second commercial. Read it loudly and with enthusiasm.

A THIRTY-SECOND COMMERCIAL TO ME

_____, I am great!

I am a unique individual, a new kind of person the world has never known before. I was born to do well. I was born to succeed. I was born to bless others' lives. I was born to be great because I've got what it takes to be great.

I am a child of God.

I am enthusiastic.

I am optimistic.

I am a change-embracer.

I am a giver, not a taker.

I am organized.

I am a hard worker.

I am happy.

I am a master of myself.

I am a leader.

I am a big thinker.

And, blessed as I am with all of these talents, there is not a thing in the world I can't do. With my God as my partner, I will never fail.

_____, go out and have a super-fantastic™ day!

Make a copy of this commercial. Delete any phrase or words you feel uncomfortable with; feel free to add additional statements that are special to you. Frame it and hang it on a wall where you can read it once every day.

ATTITUDE TUNE-UP #2

During one of my many trips, I met a man who gave me a card. "Read this every day and make every day a great day," he said. This should be your midday affirmation to recharge your battery. Read it aloud—and help make your whole day a great day.

OPTIMISTS' CREED

I promise myself . . .

> To be so strong that nothing can disturb my peace of mind.

> To talk health, happiness, and prosperity to every person I meet.

> To make all my friends feel there is something in them.

> To look at the sunny side of everything and make my optimism come true.

> To think only of the best, to work only for the
>   best and to expect only the best.
>
> To be just as enthusiastic about the success of
>   others as I am about my own.
>
> To forget the mistakes of the past and press on to
>   the greater achievements of the future.
>
> To wear a cheerful countenance at all times and
>   give every living creature I meet a smile.
>
> To give so much time to the improvement of
>   myself that I have no time to criticize others.
>
> To be too large for worry, too noble for anger,
>   too strong for fear, and too happy to permit
>   the presence of trouble.

This was given to me after a speech I gave to the Optimists' Club in Atlanta, Georgia

■   ATTITUDE TUNE-UP #3

Since physiologists say the subconscious mind is most
receptive right before we fall asleep and right after we
wake up, instead of watching the news or complaining
when you wake up, use those minutes more construc-
tively. End your day by reading your own personal
affirmations. Remember that affirmations are strong,
positive statements about you that you believe or want

to believe. You may not believe them today, but if you repeat them enough, you **will** believe them. Let me start the list for you:

I am important.

I love myself unconditionally.

I am a good person.

I have many good qualities to offer.

It's okay to make a mistake.

I deserve to be happy.

I respect myself.

I am a caring person.

I am capable and confident.

I am handling my problems effectively each day.

I am prepared to do my best.

I walk by faith, not by sight.

Finally, read the book that is the world's number one best-seller, and 100% guaranteed to inspire and motivate you with thousands of great stories and affirmations: *the Bible.*

Don't forget: The best coach with the strongest power over your performance is the coach that lives within you.

—*Keith D. Harrell*

QUOTES FOR YOUR ATTITUDE

Make the most of yourself, for that is all there is of you.

—Ralph Waldo Emerson

It's not what you are that holds you back . . . it's what you think you are not.

—Denis Waitley

Always do your best. What you plant now, you will harvest later.

—Og Mandino

 **ecommended
eading List**

for

Chapter 5

The Power in You
by Wally "Famous" Amos and
Gregory Amos

The Magic of
Thinking Big
by David J. Schwartz, Ph.D.

Understanding Your
Potential
by Myles Munroe, Ph.D.

6

IS YOUR
ATTITUDE SHOWING?

*Your attitude today determines
your success tomorrow.*

—Keith D. Harrell

Sometimes a potential catastrophe can force you to face your attitude. For example I had worked almost fourteen years with Big Blue (IBM). One Friday afternoon they called us all in for a *major* announcement. About 650 of us were crammed into an auditorium and we felt it in our bones . . . something big—and probably bad—was up.

The marketing director didn't pull any punches: IBM was laying off 40,000 employees worldwide. That meant 80% of the 650 in that auditorium wouldn't be around within six months. The marketing director wished us a good weekend. In the dead silence that followed, we could all feel the defeat and helplessness. The vibes in the room were clear: self-confidence and positive attitude were going down the tubes.

Being a consciously committed, proactive, positive thinker, I stood up, raised my hand and shouted, "I'VE GOT A QUESTION." The director, puzzled, acknowledged me and gave me the floor. "Once this 80% is gone, can I get a bigger office? One with a window view?" Everyone burst into laughter. They weren't surprised; I was the resident optimist and they knew I always looked for the bright side.

A good friend standing next to me nudged me and said, "You'll probably be the first to go." I was.

I kept smiling, walking briskly with a spring in my step throughout the whole process of losing my job and struggling with the next step. I didn't always feel like it, but what I never lost was the knowledge that staying positive and looking forward would get me through it all a lot easier than if I succumbed to negative feelings.

How's Your Attitude?

Is your negative attitude showing? Do you often look depressed? Do you often walk with a slow, defeated pace? Do you often fail to make eye contact with the person you are talking to? Do you exhibit a look of anger or frustration when things don't go your way? Do you pout as a way of expressing your negative opinion?

If you answered *yes* to any of these questions, perhaps your negative attitude *is* showing and negatively affecting others. The nonverbal expression of your attitude could be holding you back from making the winning first impression you need to achieve your ultimate success.

Dr. Ed Metcalf, a professional speaker and trainer from the Metcalf Group, based in Roswell, Georgia, speaks on the topic of nonverbal communication: "Realize that your body language mirrors your verbal language. Remember, that body language reflects feelings, not facts. More than 70% of our communication is nonverbal." That's right—70%. Even without our speaking, our body language broadcasts our attitudes—and has a powerful way of telling someone what our thoughts or desires may be.

Most people make quick judgments and form fast opinions based on a person's nonverbal behavior. Normally, within minutes we try to decide whether a person is good or bad, honest or threatening, happy or sad. We form some kind of opinion based on a person's walk, facial expression, or overall body gestures. We form some kind of attitude toward that person based on what we perceive as their attitude as exhibited by their body language. Of all the things a person wears, the most important is his or her expression. Remember, a smile causes the brain to release a flood of chemicals that make you feel good.

Dr. Mary Chestnut, a psychologist based in Atlanta, Georgia, says that "Our own external expressions play a major role in helping trigger our own internal emotions." The research is too compelling to ignore: Optimism, positive thinking, affirmations, and visualizing all contribute to our mental and physical health. Working to develop positive external body language should go hand in hand with the affirming self-coaching we discussed in the last chapter. Let's get those face muscles working in a smile. Now, walk tall, proud and with energy. Inside, you may not feel like bouncing and smiling, but the outside expression of health and happiness will turn things around if you do it—and keep on doing it.

I learned an important lesson about how a person's expressions can alter the direction of a situation after having the following experience:

Atlanta traffic can be fierce. Several years ago, I got into bumper-to-bumper traffic heading up an I-285 on-ramp. Nobody was moving in front of me, but as I looked in my rear-view mirror I saw a car coming up behind me . . . and it wasn't slowing down. I tried slowing it down by talking positively to it. It didn't work. The car's tires screeched as they tried to keep from running into me. I knew the car was going to plow into me, but it just tapped my rear bumper. No damage to me or the car, but I was shouting and beating on my horn. "You ought to be wearing glasses, lady!" I screamed at the driver. Suddenly she leaned over her steering wheel and blew me a big kiss. I thought for a moment: "I'm single, let me be positive." I blew her a kiss back. Despite all my shouts and body language, this woman blew one kiss—a small whimsical gesture. Thus she altered my reaction and inspired me to keep from turning the situation into an unpleasant scene. When the traffic cleared up we both drove off smiling.

TUNE-UP YOUR POSITIVE ATTITUDE EXPRESSIONS

Here is an exercise to help tune-up your nonverbal communication: sit up straight and smile. Think of something or someone who is or has been a positive force in your life and hold the thought for thirty seconds. The power of a smile and the power of a positive thought have the ability to influence your emotions. Note how your emotions affect your attitude.

Let's take a deeper look at two nonverbal activities that have a great effect on how your attitude communicates itself to others: *smiling* and *walking*.

◖ ATTITUDE TUNE-UP #1

SMILING

My grandmother, who is 89 years young, has always said that people who smile more live longer. Several scientific studies in recent years have demonstrated that Grandmother was ahead of her time in her analysis.

1. Do you smile at yourself?
2. Do you smile at people?
3. Do you smile only when someone smiles back at you?
4. Do you smile only when things are going well?

If you answered "No" to Questions 1 and 2, remember that smiling greatly influences your internal emotions, even if you have to force yourself to find something to smile about.

For the next 21 days, focus on one thought a day that will make you smile. Keep this thought running through your mind and practice smiling ten times a day.

If you answered "Yes" to Questions 3 and 4, remember: To be the best, you must be prepared at all times to give your best. Don't wait for someone to smile at you first. Smile at everyone, knowing that if people don't have a smile, you can give them yours.

☐ ATTITUDE TUNE-UP #2

WALKING

Walking is a wonderful way to demonstrate an upbeat, winning attitude. By picking up your pace in life and walking faster, you trigger the emotions to generate enthusiasm. People often make judgments of others who move too slowly or too fast.

Think of two healthy people working for the same employer. The first person trudges through the office, always taking his time. The other person has a spring to his fast-paced walk, often even faster than what might seem to be "normal." Your perception of the person walking faster might be that he is doing something important or going somewhere special. He makes you feel that he has a *purpose*. What thoughts would you have of the slow-moving person, even though he might be doing the same amount of work? Although our judgments may be incorrect, we need to recognize the image that walking speed projects. While some people may have disabilities or physical problems that control their

*I would rather begin
at the bottom and
climb to the top than to
start at the top and have
to remain there.*

—*Author Unknown*

pacing, many can project a ready smile and a sharp response in other movements that evidence the same attitude.

Consider this story of the lion and the gazelle. Every morning on the African continent, a gazelle wakes up. It knows it must run faster than the fastest lion or it will be killed. Every morning a lion wakes up. It knows it must outrun the slowest gazelle or it will starve to death. It doesn't matter whether you are a lion or a gazelle. What is important is that you had better be running when the sun comes up.

Start today by smiling and picking up your pace and watch your energy level change.

What you've done and where you've been do not matter. What really matters is in what direction you are going and how you take yourself there.

—*Keith D. Harrell*

QUOTES FOR YOUR ATTITUDE

You're either *on* the way or *in* the way.
You're either saying hello or goodbye.

—Les Brown

If better is possible, good is not enough.

—Author Unknown

It's a funny thing about life: If you
refuse to accept anything but the very
best, you will very often get it.

—W. Somerset Maugham

*R*ecommended *R*eading List

for

Chapter 6

Getting Your Message Across
by Kurt Hanks

Sound Bites
by Kathy Kerchner

Presentations Plus
by David A. Peoples

Enthusiasm is the mainspring of the soul. Keep it wound up and you will never be without power to get what you actually need.

—*Author Unknown*

ENTHUSIASM
POWERFUL ATT

Enthusiasm means puttin
in motion.

—*Kei*

Where does the word *enthusiasm* come from? The English word *enthusiasm* is derived from the Greek *enthousiasmos*, which means "inspiration." The two root words are *enthous* and *entheos*, which mean "God or spirit within."

Without question, enthusiasm is a vital element in maintaining a positive attitude. Enthusiasm **is** an attitude. Enthusiasm is to attitude what breathing is to life. Enthusiasm enables you to make do with what you have and engages the spirit that moves within.

Enthusiasm has always played an important role in my life, even when I was a child. When I was nine years old, I made the final cut for Little League baseball, but I didn't get a uniform—just a hat. I was so proud that I wore the hat to bed for the next three months. I didn't get to play. I just sat on the bench, but the whole experience was a highlight for me because I was part of the team.

One day I asked my coach, "Sarge, how did I make the team? I am only nine years old. I know there are older and better players who could have helped the team." Sarge replied, "It was your enthusiasm and your spirit for doing whatever it took just to be part of the team. Even though you won't play much this year, I know that if your positive attitude and your team spirit rub off, we can win the championship. One day you'll get your chance to play." He nurtured me, advising me to watch the others play because one day I would be out there. He was right. From age 11 to 12, I was a Little League all-star.

To give another example from my childhood, I used to play baseball with Darrel, the little boy across the street. Although Darrel was about three years younger than I was, I often went over to his house after school to play with him. His father had died when Darrel was younger; all he had were his sister, Shawn, and their mother. Darrel didn't have any other children around to play with, and he would get extremely excited when I would come to play.

Darrel's enthusiasm for life was second to none. It didn't matter to him what we played. In fact, he didn't know how to play most games I suggested, and he seldom won at any game. However, his excitement at being recognized, his excitement at participating, and his excitement at learning were a blessing for us both. Darrel's enthusiasm made a difference, and it influenced my attitude.

Darrel's story is proof that enthusiasm is contagious. For those of you who have children around you, notice the magic they display. The spirit within—their enthusiasm for life—is a gift we must all recapture. As I tell people in my seminars, *never let the kid in you die.* Never lose sight of the little things that make you laugh, that rekindle your spirit. Remember, you may grow old, but you never have to grow too old to enjoy life.

During a speaking engagement in Orlando, Florida, I met a woman named Pam who shared a story about her three-year-old son, Drew. Pam and Drew were walking through a park when he looked down and pointed to a broken tree branch lying on the ground. His mother responded, "Honey, that is only a stick," but Drew became so excited that he picked up the branch and said, "Mom, take a closer look. This is not just any stick. Think of all the things we can do with this. This is a *real* stick."

Recently in one of my seminars in Atlanta, Georgia I met a woman named Cindy Campbell, one of the most enthusiastic people I know. A few years ago, a head-on car collision put her into a coma for two months and left her with a skull fracture, collapsed lungs, and compound fractures of both arms and her right leg and hip. Through long months of hospitalization and extensive therapy, she learned anew how to breathe and move and talk. Cindy had loving parents who saw her through this crisis, but she also had "a positive, hopeful attitude and God watching over me. I am absolutely convinced they are responsible for my successful recovery and rehabilitation." Cindy still walks a little slowly today, but overcoming these great blows kindled an enthusiasm in her to face each day with renewed spirit and thanks.

When I talk about enthusiasm in my seminars, I ask my audience three questions: *Where do you buy it? How do you get it? How much does it cost?* I then do an exercise in which I divide the audience into two or three groups, depending on the audience size. I challenge them to make noise, to let it go, to let out all of their enthusiasm for a full five seconds.

I even turn this into a contest, telling them the loudest group will get a prize. What group do you think makes the most noise? The last group. It never fails. If there are three groups, the second group does slightly better than the first, but the last group always uses every ounce of their collective enthusiasm to give an outstanding effort.

Why is it that adults wait to compete before giving their best? After the exercise, most adults want another chance, which lets me remind them of the old adage that you never get a second chance to make a first impression.

Ironically, when I give this same exercise to children, there is no differentiation between groups. What group would you say wins? They all do. The first group is just as loud as the last group. Children don't care who is watching. They love a challenge; they love to let it go.

My friend, Dr. Metcalf, shared with me the thought that enthusiasm is sharing what you have inside yourself with others. For me, enthusiasm is an internal spirit that speaks out through your actions, from your commitment and your belief in what you are doing.

Enthusiasm is not always a given, however. There have been times in my life when I lacked the commitment, action, and spirit needed to achieve success. A time that really sticks out in my mind was three weeks after finishing my college basketball career at Seattle University. At that point, I should have been committed to improving my basketball skills and preparing myself to do whatever it took to get ready to go after my life-long goal of playing in the NBA. I realize now that I wasn't committed. I didn't really do anything to enhance my skills or improve my draft position. I adopted the *attitude* that if I get drafted, I'll take action—I'll make a commitment then. Looking back, it's easy to see what was missing. What was really missing was my commitment and consequently my faith, spirit and enthusiasm. There are situations in all our lives that get us down, but it is the power of our enthusiasm, our internal spirit, and our faith that enables us to bounce back.

—Enthusiasm gives you the power to get up early when you are not a morning person.

—Enthusiasm keeps you working on a project and keeps you from quitting.

—Enthusiasm gives you the courage to take the risks needed for success.

—Enthusiasm fuels motivation to make things happen.

—Enthusiasm brightens your personality.

—Enthusiasm combats fear and worry.

—Enthusiasm distinguishes a championship team from an average team.

—Enthusiasm is the fire in the belly that says
  don't wait.

—Enthusiasm is the burning desire that communicates commitment, determination, and
  spirit. It shows everyone else that you are
  sold on what you are doing and that you are
  seriously motivated.

—Enthus**iasm** allows me to understand that the
  last four letters mean **I A**m **S**eriously **M**otivated.

—Enthusiasm and a positive attitude are the
  winning ingredients for success.

As a professional speaker, I ask thousands of people each year: *How many people like a person who demonstrates sincere, honest enthusiasm?* The response is
deafening.

To become enthusiastic, you must act enthusiastically. I
appreciate those special people whose enthusiasm has
affected my attitude. Three people in particular who have
influenced my attitude with their enthusiasm are tennis
pro Jimmy Connors, poet Maya Angelou, and ESPN
sports commentator Dick Vitale. They are all celebrities,
and their enthusiasm is a model for everyone who has
shared their presence and excitement for what they do.

Every time I saw Jimmy Connors play in a tennis match,
his enthusiasm and passion for the game was evident
from the moment the first ball is served. I'll never forget watching the New York Open a few years ago. He

was almost 40 years old, but played with the tenacity and fire of someone much younger. The effect he had on the crowd was electrifying.

Maya Angelou has overcome great adversity in her life and still has compassion for others; it comes through loud and clear in all her works. Her passion for her work seems to transcend the pages of her writings and makes me feel as though I were right there with her.

Finally, Dick Vitale has certainly influenced how commentators broadcast sports. His enthusiasm and style make watching any sporting event a true experience!

The enthusiasm of these people for what they do is contagious. Whatever profession you're in, whatever interests you, look for those within that profession who exhibit an enthusiastic attitude to inspire you.

POSITIVE GREETINGS WITH ENTHUSIASM

The words that we use, the things that we say, have a tremendous impact on how we feel. Start using words that can uplift your attitude and the attitude of those around you. Most people greet each other with words that have no power or energy. For example: When asked how she is doing or how she feels, the average response is "I'm okay"; "I guess I'm making it"; "I'll survive"; "I'm hangin' in"; "Is it payday?"; "I don't know right now, talk to me later." One of my favorite responses was from a man I met at the Atlanta airport. When I asked how he was doing, he responded, "I'm just getting out from under things." Having some fun with this person, I said, "With that attitude, looks like you need to go back!" He laughed and said, "You're probably right!"

We should understand that the subconscious mind does not know the real experience. One important secret to internal motivation and being positive is when you're feeling somewhat down-spirited, don't tell people how you feel, *tell them how you want to feel.* By controlling what you say, using positive words with enthusiasm, you help to change your physical and mental state. Not only are the benefits self-rewarding, but you'll realize the positive impact that you'll have on others.

I personally started using my positive greeting "I feel *super-fantastic*™!" several years ago after watching an NBA commercial. I was excited when they used the word FANNNTASTIC!! to describe the NBA. It was at that moment that I decided to start saying "*Super-fantastic*™," since I exercise my NBA (Natural Born Ability) every day. While working at IBM, every time someone would walk by my office or anywhere near, and greeted me, I would respond with a big, positive "I feel *super-fantastic*™!" It wasn't long before people started to ask how I felt just to hear if I would say something else. It became so popular that if I accidentally said, "I feel great!" people would be disappointed and ask if everything was okay. Most people enjoy working and living with people who try to view life, and live life for what it is . . . a beautiful gift. I'll never forget the person in my audience who, hearing my talk on using positive responses, came up to me after my presentation. He said "Sir, I don't mean to sound negative," and I thought to myself "Well, don't." He then said, "How can you tell people that you feel super-fantastic every day? That's impossible!" I looked at him with a big smile and said, "I don't have to feel *super-fantastic*™ every day, all I have to do is feel it today! The key is if you don't feel it, you tell people how you want to feel and it won't be long before you do." The person smiled and walked away and said, "I think I got it."

■ ATTITUDE TUNE-UP #1

Take a few minutes to reflect on the people in your life who act enthusiastically and have a positive effect on your attitude.

■ ATTITUDE TUNE-UP #2

To help boost your own enthusiasm, follow this outline:

1. Count your blessings daily, and give thanks.

2. Stay focused. Don't lose sight of your target. Write a goal statement in three or four areas of your life, such as:

   a. I will walk two miles, three days a week, to become more fit.

   b. I will not let petty office politics have power over my personal or professional life.

   c. I will set aside personal time with my family members every week.

   d. If you find yourself straying, reread your statements and remind yourself why you want to stay focused.

3. Help someone less fortunate. It brings out your true spirit.

4. Trust your instincts and take action. Put yourself in motion; do *something*.

5. Never let the kid in you die. Observe children; learn to see the world through the eyes of a child.

◼ ATTITUDE TUNE-UP #3

The Fun Factor: To be enthusiastic, you must act enthusiastically. What three things do you need to do to be more enthusiastic?

◼ ATTITUDE TUNE-UP #4

Stop right now and reflect on some minor victories—things you've forgotten that were special. Rekindle the experiences that bring a smile to your face.

◼ ATTITUDE TUNE-UP #5

Create an upbeat positive greeting that builds enthusiasm. Feel free to use *Super-Fantastic*™. How are you doing?

*Do not "tell" the world
what you can do—
"show" it!
Let your actions speak
for themselves.*

—*Keith D. Harrell*

QUOTES FOR YOUR ATTITUDE

Enthusiasm is to attitude what
breathing is to life. Nothing great was
ever achieved without enthusiasm.

—Ralph Waldo Emerson

Enthusiasm is that mysterious
something that turns an average
person into an outstanding individual.

—Dr. Robert H. Schuller

Recommended Reading List *for* Chapter 7

Enthusiasm Makes the Difference
by Dr. Norman Vincent Peale

Life's Not Fair But God Is Good
by Dr. Robert H. Schuller

The Greatest Salesman in the World
by Og Mandino

8

SELF-CONFIDENCE: ANOTHER KEY TO YOUR SUCCESS

*If ye have faith . . . nothing shall
be impossible unto you.*

—*Matthew 17:20*

Do you *need* self-confidence? You bet. It doesn't matter where you're from; it doesn't matter what you do in life. If you are a parent, you need self-confidence to know you can carry your family through any adversity. If you are a child, or even a young adult, you need self-confidence in a big way: You need it to overcome peer pressure; you need it to realize your dreams; you need it to overcome the pressures of growing up in today's society.

If you are an employee, a manager, or a top executive, you need self-confidence now more than ever to endure all the change in today's work place, and to handle all the effects of downsizing, rightsizing, or capsizing. For those who may be out of work or looking for a career change, your self-confidence and your attitude will be the two forces that empower you to succeed. You must continue to grow and to protect these treasures, because they are golden.

You may have noticed that those who seem to be in control of their lives, who are upbeat and positive, have a belief that they *can*. They view themselves as successful. They have a strong sense of self, a positive self-image. Their aura of self-confidence seems to empower everyone around them.

Our attitudes and confidence are always tested. A major revelation in discovering how my self-confidence influenced my attitude occurred when I first started working for IBM as a sales representative. When I wasn't making quota and couldn't close a sale, I would start

Oliver Wendell Holmes once attended a meeting in which he was the shortest man present. "Dr. Holmes," quipped a friend, "I should think you'd feel rather small among us big fellows." "I do," retorted Holmes. "I feel like a dime among a lot of pennies."

—Oliver Wendell Holmes

doubting all my abilities and listen to negative comments from other people outside IBM—like: *Maybe you are in the wrong business*; *Maybe you shouldn't be in this business*; *Maybe it's the economy.*

It was just a matter of time before what had been a positive attitude at the start of my career transformed into a lack of confidence and a negative attitude. Luckily, it lasted only a few months because my confidence was restored by the excellent mentoring and coaching from other IBMers accompanied with a belief in myself.

Such fluctuations in self-confidence move through our lives like a roller coaster—up sometimes, down sometimes. Yet, if you lack a basic core of self-confidence, it is almost impossible to achieve success in any field. You must develop confidence. Confidence starts by believing in yourself and in your abilities.

The February 1994 issue of *Fortune* magazine listed America's most-admired corporations. IBM was ranked number 354 out of 404 companies. In the mid-80s, *Fortune* had ranked IBM as America's most-admired company, three different times. What do you think is the attitude and the confidence level of those affiliated with IBM today?

As I look back on the confidence of my colleagues when I was an IBMer, I remember that they had a strong belief in their abilities and the products, as well as a positive attitude about the services they could provide for their customers.

Recent years have brought many changes at IBM. One commercial I recently saw was built around the theme "There is no better time to do business with IBM." I believe this commercial was designed to assure people that IBM products are still a good investment, regardless of the company's fallen stock prices and downsizing, and the fierce competition from other companies. I also believe the best advertisement for IBM is not on TV or on radio, or through IBM products but through its employees' confidence in and attitude toward themselves and their company. IBMers today must look inside themselves to rekindle the fire and the self-confidence that each one of them has the power to positively impact the bottom line. Remember: In business, customers are buying *you, your* confidence, *your* attitude, and *your* ability to positively impact *their* bottom line.

Whether you're a professional businessperson or a student starting your first day of college, you need self-confidence to be a success. In the world of sports, confidence applies to both individual competition and team competition. Whether you are a coach or a player, your confidence and the confidence of those around you will ultimately affect your level of success.

Winning starts with confidence; confidence affects everyone and every service or product it comes in contact with. Winning and confidence walk hand in hand, and your starting point is your self-belief. Winning starts with you. You can't be in control of your success without self-confidence, faith and a positive attitude.

As an example, consider Bill Gates, Chairman of the Board and CEO of Microsoft Corporation. His grades in school were poor. His high school counselors called him an underachiever who often received low grades in subjects he didn't like. Yet, self-confidence aided him in formulating the plans for the Microsoft Corporation. A recent *Fortune* survey of U.S. executives selected Microsoft as the most innovative company in America and one of the most admired.

Whether we're in sports, in business or in education, our attitudes were all programmed in early stages of our lives. We're all running our lives on two basic programs: what others say to/about us, and what we say to/about ourselves. We usually give more attention and importance to negative input into our program, and negative input weakens. Phrases like, "You're not that smart," "You're too old," "You're too young," "You've never been graceful," are destructive to our self-esteem.

Abraham Lincoln lost 17 elections in a row, watched a loved one go through a nervous breakdown, and had a nervous breakdown himself—all before he became president of the United States. How many times do you think he heard something like, "Hey, Abe, you're 0 for 17. Maybe politics isn't your game." Lincoln knew, though, that failures *are* life's lessons with which we can build success in the future. Most of us learn more from these life lessons—what many people choose to call "failures"—than from any "successes" we've enjoyed.

If you think you are beaten, you are;

if you think you dare not,

you don't; if you like to win,

but you think you can't,

it is almost certain you won't.

If you think you'll lose, you've lost,

for out of the world we find

success begins with a fellow's will—

it's all in the state of mind.

If you think you are outclassed,

you are—

you've got to think high to rise.

You've got to be sure of yourself before

you can ever win a prize.

—*Adopted from a poster*
that was in the IBM sales school

If you're a parent, think about when your children took their first steps. When they stumbled and fell after that first tentative step, did anyone say, "Oh, forget it, you'll only get hurt if you keep this up?" We all know that children have to get right back up and keep on trying until walking becomes second nature. So we encourage them: "Don't worry; Mommy and Daddy will catch you. You're doing great!"

At one of his seminars in Atlanta, Georgia, I heard Zig Ziglar, a world-renowned motivational speaker, say that the word "no" is 17 times more powerful than the word "yes." Many of us are frozen in one position in life because we've heard the word "no" so often. If you've heard the word "no" once, I'll need to tell you, "Yes, you can" 17 times before you're able to cancel out the one "no." If your mind were a word processor, think of all the keystrokes you'd need to make to eliminate one little two-letter word.

So be careful what you put into your mind—or anybody else's mind. Start building your self-confidence. Start right now to begin living positively—and positively living.

■ ATTITUDE TUNE-UP #1

Below are five plans for you to enhance your confidence:

1. *Involvement*: Get involved with a group that shares interests similar to yours, and/or get involved in a charitable organization; volunteer your time in your community. By becoming involved and helping other people, you will build a sense of accomplishment and derive momentum. Involvement helps you develop a sense of purpose—confidence. I get involved every year by training and motivating the United Way staff and on-loan executives for their fund-raising campaign. This experience gives me a strong sense of accomplishment.

What are some organizations you can get involved with to help build your momentum?

List them:

2. *Motivation:* Understand what really motivates you. Life offers you two basic options: Move or be moved. What are the driving forces that enable you to go forward? The word *motive,* defined in the second edition of *The American Heritage Dictionary,* means "to cause motion." What motives are moving you toward success? One of the strongest forms of motivation is love. Think of ways to rediscover the love for what you do in both your personal and professional life. Get excited, get re-energized, and take action.

3. *Acceptance:* First, start by accepting yourself. Tell yourself it is okay to make mistakes. Success is sometimes measured by the number of tries or the number of failures we experience. Ultimately, what shapes our self-image is not so much what happens *to* us, but what happens *in* us. Take an "I can" attitude to enhance confidence, and refuse to carry leftover emotional baggage. Don't be one of those people who are always looking back and talking to Mr. or Ms. "SCB" (Shoulda, Coulda, But).

My grandmother would always say, "If you don't ever want to be depressed, don't look back." Learn to let go of past failures or mistakes—the past does not equal the future. See yourself as you will one day become. Gain more confidence by concentrating on staying positive. Your attitude communicates who you are and who you want to be. Believe in yourself. You can't be happy unless you believe in yourself; you can't accumulate riches—either material or spiritual—unless your self-image is worthy of the riches you seek. Remind yourself:

"Though it may be important to
believe in others, it is equally
important to believe
in yourself."

—Author Unknown

Keep repeating the positive self-talk suggestions from Chapter 2, constantly reminding yourself *I'd make a lousy anybody else, but I can be the best ME in the world.*

4. *Goals:* Almost everyone talks about setting life goals. Why? Because it's almost impossible to stay focused or evaluate your successes or failures (life lessons) without a purpose, an objective, and a plan. Yet, most people spend more time planning a wedding or a vacation than they do planning their lives.

Write down your life goals. Break them down into these seven areas: *Career/education; family/personal relationships; financial; personal development; physical; social; spiritual.*

Make sure they are realistic goals. Your goals should be realistic and reachable if you stick to your plan. Periodically check to see how much ground you have covered and how much more you have to go. If necessary, as time passes, restructure your plans for the steps you will take to reach a particular goal, but don't abandon the goal. You may want to reset your goal if you still want to achieve it. Having a goal helps you keep doing what you should be doing. Set goals, plan your life, and work your plan. Then your goals will lead you to the fulfillment of your dreams.

SUGGESTED PERSONAL GOALS WORKSHEET

Career/Education:

1. _____

2. _____

3. _____

Family/Personal Relationships:

1. _____

2. _____

3. _____

Financial:

1. _____

2. _____

3. _____

Personal Development:

1. _____

2. _____

3. _____

Physical:

1. _____

2. _____

3. _____

Social:

1. _____

2. _____

3. _____

Spiritual:

1. _____

2. _____

3. _____

Other:

1. _____

2. _____

3. _____

5. *Effort:* As you look to develop your self-confidence, meet with other people who are achieving success and demonstrating a high level of self-esteem. Take the initiative. Contact people you admire because of their presence and style. Look closely at people who have a positive impact on you. What are the things they are doing to gain success? What do you need to do to achieve their level of success? What books do they read? Who are their mentors? What skills or talents have they worked to develop? How do they spend their time? Then face your biggest challenge: are you willing to pay the price? If you want success, you will be successful.

If you look at your **I**nvolvement, your **M**otivation, your **A**cceptance of yourself, your **G**oals, and the **E**ffort it takes to be successful in life, you'll see that you've just spelled the word **IMAGE**. Don't ever forget you are made in an image of greatness. It's self-confidence that helps build a positive image of yourself. Start building *yourself—* start building your success.

QUOTES FOR YOUR ATTITUDE

Dream to be more than what you are.
You are the one who can stretch
your own horizon.

—Edgar F. Magnin

Experience is the name everyone
gives to their mistakes.

—Oscar Wilde

for
Chapter 8

The Ultimate Secrets of Total Self-Confidence
by Dr. Robert Anthony

The Ya Gottas for Success
by Larry H. Winget

Feel the Fear and Do It Anyway
by Susan Jeffers, Ph.D.

9

Acceptance of Change Depends on Attitude

*The only thing you can change is
yourself, but sometimes that
changes everything.*

—*Author Unknown*

Have you ever suffered from "changecosis?" Rapid heartbeat, tense muscles—you worry yourself into a tight frown just hearing the word "change?" All of us have been confronted by this syndrome at some time. What is the cure? The cure is to learn to embrace change in a positive way. I know this sounds simple, and it's not easy. It involves reprogramming your attitude and looking at new paradigms.

With all of the changes that happen so quickly in all levels of life today, you must have a positive attitude if you are to grow with change and embrace that growth. The only thing in life *you can be sure you can change* is *you*.

To be successful today, you must be a change-embracer, and you must stay in a change mode. If you're not a change-embracer, how do you start to become one? The first step is to recognize and accept that you may have changecosis. This potentially life-threatening disease can't effectively be addressed or diagnosed by others. Change-cosis must be self-diagnosed, and it involves admitting that you are resisting change.

I had a long, serious bout of changecosis which involved my six-foot-seven height. I had spent most of my young adulthood chasing a dream to become a professional basketball player. In high school, I was an All-American and was voted Most Valuable Player of our championship team. I accepted a scholarship to Seattle University, where I played for four years, three during which I was the captain. I ended my senior year averaging over

16 points per game. In June 1979 I expected to be drafted by some professional team in the National Basketball Association. I had dreamed of being drafted by the NBA for 12 years and everyone I knew also expected that I would be. The day of the draft, I waited and waited and waited . . . but the phone did not ring.

I was devastated. I had to give up almost a full lifetime of planning, working and dreaming. I felt cheated, and I didn't want to talk about it. The bitterness was made fresh every time someone commented on my height, and it usually ended with, "You must play pro basketball." For a long time I choked back the bitterness, until one day I suddenly let it go. I decided to embrace this major change and focus on being positive. I realized that for me to grow inwardly I had to move on with my life. Now, when someone asks me about my unfulfilled dream of not playing professional basketball, I don't feel bitterness or disappointment. For example, I remember a few years ago a woman on a plane asked me if I played with the NBA (National Basketball Association). I replied, "Yes, I do. I'm a first-round draft choice; I'm the most valuable player, and I'm owner of a team and we win the championship every year!"

"You play with the NBA?" she asked.

"Yes, I do . . . I play with my **N**atural **B**orn **A**bilities, and I'm slam dunking every day!"

It took me three years, but I managed through an unexpected and unwelcome change in my life. The next time you are faced with a difficult change, focus on staying positive and work on being a change-embracer by using all of your natural born abilities.

To embrace change, be aware there are two types of change: Planned and unplanned. If your attitude is brighter and more positive, the chances are good that you'll embrace change. Read the following questions to determine if you have changecosis. When confronted by change, do you generally become rigid? Do you over-react? Become suspicious? Begin to blame others? Deny that it bothers you? Do you experience the "Yes, but . . . " syndrome? If you answered "yes" to any of these questions, there is a good chance you have changecosis.

There are a multitude of reasons for changecosis. You may simply fear the unknown. Perhaps the rationale for the change has not been clearly communicated to you, making you feel you lack ownership in the proposed change, so you experience a loss of self-esteem. Maybe you resist change because you've previously had a bad experience, or perhaps you fear the required change demands new behaviors incongruent with your established beliefs. Whatever your reasons for resisting change, examine them.

Recently, my grandmother had a bout with resistance to change. We had just bought her a new remote-control television, and she didn't like it. I asked her why she didn't like the new set. "I don't like change," she said. After questioning her further, I found out the real reason she didn't like it was that she couldn't see the

Until you have learned to be tolerant of those who do not always agree with you—until you have cultivated the habit of saying some kind word of those whom you do not admire—until you have formed the habit of looking for the good instead of the bad there is in others, you will be neither successful nor happy.

—*Author Unknown*

buttons on the remote very well, and she frequently forgot where she left the remote. We got her an extra-large remote with buttons that light up, and then we attached it to the nightstand by her bed. Now she loves that new remote-control television! The point here is you need to carefully examine the reasons you are resisting change—your reasons may turn out to be quite "treatable."

Not all reasons for resisting change are bad, and they don't necessarily affirm that you have changecosis. For example, if you are being asked to make a change on your job that conflicts with deeply held personal principles—such as being asked to do something unethical or illegal, or just contrary to the way you feel people should treat one another—you may have reason to resist the change and may want to reevaluate your job situation. Remember, the power of choice belongs to *you*.

However, focus attention on those instances in which resistance to change is based on excuses rather than on legitimate reasons. If you usually react to any change in a negative or a counterproductive manner, you probably have changecosis.

RESPONSES TO CHANGE

Most people respond to change in one of *four ways*. For example, at IBM, when we first heard we were downsizing some people had a *neutral* response. In other words, they thought the rumored changes would not happen or would be too minor to have a lasting impact. Others viewed the change *negatively*, disagreeing with the entire change process whether they understood it or not. They rejected the need to change and complained excessively about all proposals.

Some people had actively *counterproductive* attitudes. For example, in one department where employees knew their head count would be cut 30% in only six months, some workers' attitudes were, "Well, I'm not going to do much for the next six months until I know I'm going to have a job." When they responded to change in this fashion, their response deliberately undermined the change and may have further jeopardized their futures.

The IBMers who accepted change *positively,* however, showed that they possessed a healthy attitude toward change. They exercised their power of choice and responded to the change in an affirming manner. This does not mean they didn't have concerns, but by exercising the power of choice, they determined their response to change and the challenges it brings.

The key to responding to change is to *affirm it. You* control the change situation, rather than allowing the change situation to control *you* and disrupt your entire life. Accepting change is more likely to occur when you believe you can successfully conquer the challenges created by the new change. You must look inside yourself to see the benefits of the change and to understand that where there is change, there will be growth.

ACCEPTING CHANGE

We can't always control the inevitability of change, but we *can* control our responses. The only fact we know about change is that it will continue. Only when our attitude toward change becomes positive and we learn to view change as an opportunity, will we begin to unleash our full potential. When confronted by change, replace the change-resistant behaviors with the following change-embracing behaviors:

1. Face the reality of change. Convert a threat into an opportunity.

2. Acknowledge that you need to change. Be a solution to a problem, not a problem.

3. Create ownership of the change. Have a vision for your role in the change process.

4. Break the desired change into small increments. Start with the easiest part of the change so that success is likely in the beginning and can inspire you to continue working toward new goals.

5. Develop a sense of presence about change. Avoid delaying tactics.

6. When possible, work on only one major change at a time. Keep the rest of your life balanced.

7. Write an affirmation of the change as if it has already occurred. Post your affirmation where it can be seen readily and often. Here are some examples of such affirmations:
   • I have the skills to make my life a success.
   • I will be the best worker in my new department.

   For instance, if you're worried about losing your job because your company is downsizing, phrase your affirmations like this:
   • New jobs and opportunities are presenting themselves to me.

8. Be patient. True change comes from within. It takes time and effort.

9. Accept change on your terms. Remember, *you* control your response.

10. Seek out support systems.

11. Celebrate each successful step taken, no matter how small.

We are more likely to resist those changes imposed by others. The changes that are most easily accepted are those in our control and of a personal decision. We readily embrace those changes we perceive will make us happy or have a beneficial outcome, although even with planned change, we often delay initiating the needed changes until we are in a crisis situation.

In those situations in which we don't readily embrace change, either we think that we lack the ability to implement the change, or we don't understand the change. For some of us it may be that we don't believe in the change, or we don't see the rationale for the change. When we view change as a natural part of the growth process, we activate the power of choice and take a positive response to change. Therefore, if you perceive you lack the ability or skills to handle a change, acquire those skills. If you don't understand the change, seek clarification. If you don't believe the change is needed, search your feelings: are you making excuses, or do you have legitimate concerns?

If you had taken me to lunch during my first five years with IBM, you would have had an earful of what *didn't* happen. I would have complained about why so-and-so had been promoted and I had not; I would have spouted off about not having been treated fairly; I would have griped that I didn't have a better territory. I was just plain complaining. Finally, I woke up and said, "How can I be a change-embracer?" I wanted to grow beyond where I was that day. I realized I wouldn't get far with all the leftover baggage I was carrying, so I cut it loose. We need to let go of whatever is holding us back.

Are you afraid to leave your comfort zone, or are you afraid to learn something new? Examine your feelings, discover your motives, and then begin to respond with a positive attitude.

Change is a continuous, never-ending process. It cannot—and should not—be avoided. How will you handle change in the future? Will you continue to exhibit change-resistant behaviors and never achieve your full potential, or will you become a change-embracer and discover a whole world of hidden possibilities and growth? Begin to accept change with a positive attitude.

> *The choice is yours.*
> *Change is the essence of life.*
> *Embrace it.*
>
> *—Keith D. Harrell*

ATTITUDE TUNE-UP #1

ACTION PLAN FOR PERSONAL GROWTH THROUGH PERSONAL CHANGE

Attitude Check:

1. What change needs to be accepted or initiated?

2. What major change-resistant behavior may be hindering your acceptance or initiation of change?

3. What strategy for addressing the change-resistant behavior would make it easier for you to accept or initiate change?

◼ ATTITUDE TUNE-UP #2

Attitude Required:

1. What coping skills/attitude might help you more easily embrace the needed change?

2. What empowering belief may help strengthen the decision to accept or initiate change?

3. What disempowering belief do you need to discard to facilitate accepting or initiating change?

● ATTITUDE TUNE-UP #3

Attitude Strategy:

1. Identify one strategy that may enhance acceptance or initiation of the change you selected.

2. Identify the support systems you may need to be put into place to help solidify the change.

QUOTES FOR YOUR ATTITUDE

You cannot fix what you will not face.

—James Baldwin

If you are on a road to nowhere,
find another road.

—Ashanti Proverb

Make sure your positive seeds are
planted in positive ground.

—Keith D. Harrell

*The best compensation
for doing things
is the ability to do more.*

—*Adopted from a banner*

*R*ecommended *R*eading List
for
Chapter 9

Awaken the Giant Within
by Anthony Robbins

Overcoming Resistance
by Jerald M. Jellison

I Want to Change But I Don't Know How!
by Tom Rusk, MD, and
Randy Read, MD

10

DIFFERENCES THAT MAKE
A DIFFERENCE:
IT'S ALL ABOUT ATTITUDE

*"Patience is not the ability to
wait, but the attitude
while you're waiting."*

—Keith D. Harrell

Today's challenges and opportunities for individuals and organizations are extraordinary and are unlike any challenges of the past. In the workplace and at school there is an increased demand for commitment, innovation, and productivity. To prosper in the future we must value, understand, and better utilize the wonderful diversity of people within our organizations, our schools, and our society. The dimensions of human differences impact our attitude, our behavior, and ultimately our personal and professional success.

Given today's complex society, we must realize everyone does not practice the same religion, celebrate the same holidays or share the same ideas or attitudes. All of us have been culturally programmed, and that program determines our behavior, our attitudes, and our performance. The cultural programming of our attitude determines how we react to the people and to the situations we encounter. As we move from a culture that once demanded sameness and required assimilation to one that recognizes diversity and multiculturalism, our ability to adapt to and embrace this culture will determine our success in life and in business.

When we think of managing the diversity that impacts our lives, we generally think of racial or ethnic diversity. However, diversity is about *all* our differences. Those differences can include not only racial and ethnic but also gender, sexual orientation, martial status, physical/mental, economic, religious, educational, or political. As we strive to grow, to improve, and to de-

*Progress is impossible
without change;
and those who cannot
change their minds,
cannot change anything.*

—George Bernard Shaw

velop an attitude that will propel us to success beyond the new millennium, we must discontinue old practices of either ignoring the differences of others or considering the differences to be irrelevant or inferior.

I've spoken to many companies and organizations that are making a positive difference in the lives of their employees—companies like LensCrafters, Milliken, Yellow Freight, Miller Professional Imaging, Amway, American Express, Intel, US West, Mary Kay and the Marriott Hotels, to name a few.

I read an article in *The Arizona Republican*'s business section by Max Jarman, dated March 8, 1998. It was entitled, "Employee networks are helping firms recognize diversity." Think about that. Organizations that bring people together to network, to share their differences, to recognize diversity are the ones that will have long-term success. Those are the organizations that make the biggest difference in our society.

For example, American Express has set up a support group for employees who are over the age of forty. The Intel Corporation has allowed employees to form a Christian group to help those people who want to pray and worship together before and after work. They have also enabled diverse groups to participate in an annual cultural fair in which individual cultural groups set up booths to educate other employees about their cultures and traditions. The key to teamwork among diverse people is education. The key is letting people have a chance to educate other people about their differences; and when you educate people, you give everyone an opportunity to share differences, which brings them closer and which in turn builds teamwork and success.

Consider the people who have made a difference in this world, past and present. They have all come from different backgrounds, different places of the world, different societies and different organizations, and they have had different goals and ideas. The one thing they *did* have in common was an attitude that recognized their uniqueness.

Successful organizations and fast-growing companies put people first. They allow people to network and to learn about each other. They recognize the importance of using the talents and skills of all people, regardless of color, gender, age, or physical challenges. It's no secret that success starts with the right attitude. In business, this philosophy starts at the top—with upper management; in life, it starts with *you*.

It's okay to be different, whether you're working in corporate America, going to school, or living or working in another part of the world. It's okay to be different. Your difference combined with a positive attitude will help you make the greatest difference in your life and the lives of those around you.

Do you remember the first time you felt "different?" As adults we sometimes forget how the impact of being different affected our attitudes towards ourselves, and how those attitudes impacted our behavior towards others. I was five years old and in kindergarten when I realized for the first time I was different. I was the tallest child in the class and, you may recall, I stuttered. I remember distinctly how I felt as other children pointed at me and whispered behind my back. In the United States, a country that did not celebrate differences, the "melting pot" in which everyone was supposed to be the same, I felt out of place, hurt, and confused. I did not feel as though I belonged. This early memory of being different had nothing to do with the fact that I was an African-American male; there were other African-American children in my class. Rather, my height and my physical handicap set me apart from other children, and this separateness had a great impact on my attitude and behavior. If not for the positive influences in my life at that time—my mother and my teacher— who assured me that my differences made me special, I wonder how my life would have been today. Who would I have become?

I reflected on this question as I read an article, "Athlete Ignores Limits," in the August 19, 1996, *USA Today*. The article described an outstanding athlete who was competing in the Paralympic Games. His name was Tony Volpentest. Tony was born without feet, and his right leg was three inches shorter than his left leg. Despite his limitations, Volpentest had become one of the top athletes competing in the games, dubbed as the fastest in the world. From an early age he had been driven to tackle every challenge and to try any sport by strapping on a pair of prosthetic legs and feet. What if his parents had set limitations on him instead of encouraging him? What would have happened if his teachers had refused to allow him to participate in activities with the other, able-bodied children and ignored his strengths because of these physical challenges, or if his coaches had believed the obstacles were too much for Tony to overcome? Had this happened, I would have never been allowed the privilege of being inspired by such a great athlete, and the world would have never known this inspiring individual, who had overcome severe differences to succeed in life. Clearly, his family and teachers provided the positive attitudes that so impacted Tony's life. He was encouraged and made to feel special, and he consequently believed there were no obstacles he could not overcome. He was motivated to do whatever it took to succeed.

On a personal note, when I think of the many people who are physically challenged but overcome their "limitations," I think about my cousin, Orlando Lombard. Orlando was involved in a car accident his senior year in college that robbed him of the use of both his legs. Orlando refused to be pitied or to pity himself. He lived life with zest and a positive attitude. Orlando not only refused to feel sorry for himself, he also refused to let others who had suffered spinal cord injuries wallow in pity. Time and again he responded to calls from disturbed family members or medical personnel seeking his assistance by giving hope to those who had suffered debilitating injuries similar to his. Never once did he fail to respond. He was there with his attitude—encouraging, motivating, inspiring, and doing everything in his power to ensure that no one would give up.

Sometimes a personal or company tragedy will show you what kind of person you are or what kind of company you work for. I read an article in *Business Week* by David Greising, dated February 27, 1995, about Milliken & Company, one of the largest textile companies in the world based in LaGrange, Georgia. A terrible fire had wiped out their carpet-making facility. The LaGrange plant had flared up on January 31, 1995. The next day, however, the company promised jobs for as many of its employees as possible and unemployment benefits for the rest. Two weeks later 600 of the plant's 720 employees had filled new positions at Milliken's facilities, some as far away as Britain and Japan. The company's attitude clearly showed that Milliken cared about its people. Some companies would have used this disaster to lay off or downsize their organizations. However, when Roger Milliken learned the facility was totally destroyed, he said to the employees, "We have a terrible problem. It's also a tremendous opportunity— the opportunity to show our customers, our community, and the world just how good we can be." They did just that: Milliken rebuilt its carpet-making facility in six months—a task, construction experts said, that would normally take more than two years. Talk about a speedy bounce-back. The Milliken story drives home an old message: Nothing is impossible with the right attitude.

One final story demonstrates it doesn't matter what age a person is to make a positive difference—rather, that at any age we're all unique and we all have special gifts. Recently I met a woman by the name of Karen P. Medina at a Lanier Conference in Atlanta, Georgia. She told me she had purchased my book and cassette tape, *Attitude Is Everything* and had brought them home to Connecticut, where she read the book and began listening to my tape each morning as she drove her son to school. Her son, Lance, was five years old at the time. When he entered kindergarten he was suffering from asthma; additionally, he wore glasses and was taking dancing lessons. The other boys obviously thought he was odd. Lance felt "different," to say the least when starting out the school year.

His mother continued, "He began each morning while riding to school by saying, 'Momma put Keith in. Put Keith in.' Soon he began to memorize your presentation. He particularly loved your story about your kindergarten experience. He laughed each time he listened, and I mean deep gut laughter. He began quoting you to others.

"My favorite story of Lance and his Keith Harrell experience is when he was participating in his kindergarten play. He was playing one of the professors—the lead—when they were rehearsing a song, 'Practice makes Perfect.' Lance, having listened to your tape at least twice a day for the past several months, was quite aware of your feelings that practice makes improvement. I guess he agreed so strongly with you that he brought this to the attention of his teacher. He told her that he felt they should sing, 'Practice makes Improvement,' as Keith says. Lance also felt compelled to share your quotes with his friends. At times, they would respond, 'Who the heck is Keith?' 'Keith Harrell,' he would respond. 'You don't know Keith Harrell? *Attitude Is Everything?*'"

Even a five-year-old child has his own uniqueness and is making a positive difference. At any age we must understand our own uniqueness and learn to value and respect the differences of others. When we value individuals for their uniqueness, we can eliminate the negative impact of stereotyping. Stereotyping is often destructive. In most situations it minimizes an individual's potential, talent, and accomplishments. It also sets narrow and inflexible expectations. However, when we make an attitude shift toward valuing our differences, we begin to reap long-term benefits. Our relationships, both personal and professional, are enhanced: We reduce interpersonal conflicts; we gain flexibility and creativity; and we begin to fully use our human potential.

How, then, do we begin to shift our attitudes to valuing differences in other people?

> Acknowledge differences that make people unique.
>
> Learn to value differences by focusing on the gains and seeing the positive aspects of those differences.

Walk the talk! Listen to, consider, and implement
suggestions from others.

Acknowledge and reward positive, inclusive
behavior—from yourself and from others.

Learn from your experiences, and learn from
others.

Valuing the differences in others will be one of the greatest tools to propel yourself well beyond the new millennium. An attitude of inclusiveness is more than just
a moral imperative; it's a strategic advantage.

Individuals who embrace differences of others and learn
to value those differences are the ones who will be the
most creative, resourceful, and productive in their personal lives and in their work arenas. When you begin
to look at differences that can unify instead of divide,
focusing on the positive and recognizing that any change
is uncomfortable at first, you will experience success.

◼ ATTITUDE TUNE-UP #1

Think about the first time you felt "different." Write down
your memories of the situation. What were the feelings
with being different? List those feelings.

Many feelings we associated with being different were
negative and did not make us feel good about the experience. Take a few minutes to reflect about individu-

als in your life who may seem different to you. What can you do to help their experience become a positive one? How would doing so impact your attitude and your performance? If your personal experience was positive, try to reflect on what made it positive, and apply the same principles.

◼ ATTITUDE TUNE-UP #2

List three stereotypes you may have towards particular groups (i.e., younger or older employees, ethnic or racial groups, the physically or mentally challenged).

1.

2.

3.

How have these stereotypes impacted your behavior towards that group?

What can you do to change your impression?

During the next week, read about, learn about, and become familiar with information about individuals who belong to that (or those) group(s). Challenge your stereotypes and replace old information with new facts that will impact positively your attitude and behavior toward those groups.

QUOTES FOR YOUR ATTITUDE

Wisdom is better than strength.

—Ecc. 9:16

Before taking steps, the wise man knows
the object and end of his journey.

—W. E. Du Bois

Success is the result of perfection,
hard work, learning from failure,
loyalty, and persistence.

—U.S. Ret. Gen. Colin Powell

*R*ecommended *R*eading List

for

Chapter 10

Smart Women, Smart Choices
by Hattie Hill

You Can Make It Happen
by Stedman Graham

Seven Habits of Highly Effective Families
by Stephen Covey

11

ATTITUDE TUNE-UP

Ask, and it shall be given you;
seek, and ye shall find; knock,
and it shall be opened unto you.

—*Matthew 7:7*

Enthusiasm is to attitude what breathing is to life. It's the fire in the belly. If you have no fire; maybe your wood is wet.

—Keith D. Harrell

Throughout this book, I have given you information and tips on tuning up your attitude. This chapter will summarize that information and provide you with a 21-day attitude plan.

The purpose of tuning up anything in life is to improve performance. The purpose of tuning up your attitude is to improve your success in both your personal and your professional endeavors. I challenge you to use this information—and perform the daily exercises—over the next 21 days to ensure yourself a winning attitude.

Start by analyzing your attitude toward the important challenges you face. Based on your past experiences, on past programming and the way you have been conditioned, your attitude is in one of four attitude stages—neutral, negative, counterproductive, or positive. Complete the following chart to see the area or areas in your life on which you need to focus.

ATTITUDE DISCOVERY CHART

	Neutral	Negative	Counter-Productive	Positive
Career or Education				
Family/Personal Relationships				
Financial Situation				
Personal Development				
Physical Condition				
Social or Community Involvement				
Spiritual Life				

Take aim at those areas in which you need to improve your performance and bolster your confidence. Tune-up your attitude by reciting—and following—the action steps in these exercises.

Day 1

Today I will start to tune up my attitude by studying—really studying—my chart and focusing on the areas I need to improve.

Day 2

Today I will tune up my attitude, reviewing what I learned in Chapter 2—that the loudest voice I hear is my own and that psychologists estimate that 80% of my self-talk is negative. I will control my life—I will control what I think and say to myself. I will get a journal and make a conscious effort to take notes, writing down any negative self-talk. I will then revise or rephrase those statements into positive ones. I will concentrate today on using positive self-talk. I will remember that the most important coach is the coach who lives within me.

Day 3

Today I will tune up my attitude by teaming up with other positive people. I will make a "dream team" list of positive people I want to get to know. This list will grow as I grow. My attitude will be tuned up, not by how many people are on the list, but by how many people I actually make an effort to meet and get to know. I will team up!

Day 4

Today I will tune up my attitude by inspiring others. My goal is to tell at least three people something good that I have noticed about their efforts and their attitude. I will remember that the words *I am proud of you* are very powerful. I will tune up my attitude by making an effort to tune up someone else's.

Day 5

Today I will tune up my attitude by taking a one-minute (at least) vacation to think about someone or something in my life that means more to me than anything else in the world. For a full thirty seconds, I will wear a big smile on my face while looking up and holding on to one thought. By holding this thought and by my big smile, my feelings and emotions will change, for I know that my thoughts and expressions impact my feelings, my emotions, and my attitude.

Day 6

Today I will tune up my attitude by transforming all of my stumbling blocks into stepping stones. Today I will make friends with my past. I will repeat out loud: "My past and my present help to impact my future."

*No matter what you do
in life, if you have a positive
attitude, you'll always
be 100%.
According to our alphabet system,
if you assign a numerical value
to each letter (1–26), "attitude" will
equal 100%.*

A	=	*1*
T	=	*20*
T	=	*20*
I	=	*9*
T	=	*20*
U	=	*21*
D	=	*4*
E	=	*5*
		100%

Day 7

Today I will tune up my attitude by celebrating my uniqueness. I was born to make a difference. I will not compare myself to others. I know that comparing myself to other people is a sign of low self-esteem. My new motto is: "I will make a lousy anybody else, but I can make the best *me* in the world."

Day 8

Today I will tune up my attitude by putting my goals into motion. I will start by clapping when I wake up, singing in the shower, and smiling. I will be committed today to pursuing my goals. I will not take today or any other day for granted. Today, when anyone asks me how I am doing, I will greet them with my other new motto: "I feel *super-fantastic*™!" (Or, create your own motto.)

Day 9

Today I will tune up my attitude by making a commitment to never deprive anyone of hope. It might be all they have. I realize that hope is a powerful motivator. Giving hope and encouragement is something I enjoy.

Day 10

Today I will tune up my attitude by making sure I leave everything a little bit better than I found it. I will not complain or blame others. I will give my best effort in the hope of making a difference in somebody's life— even in my own.

Day 11

Today I will tune up my attitude by promising myself to never be afraid to say, "I'm sorry." I also know that saying "I'm sorry" does not give me permission to hurt other people's feelings, but if I do, I promise to say "I'm sorry" with compassion.

Day 12

Today I will tune up my attitude by giving myself unconditional love. I will love myself regardless of the conditions in my life. If things are great or if things are bad, loving myself unconditionally gives me the power to grow.

Day 13

Today I will tune up my attitude by taking responsibility, being accountable, and being a change-embracer. I can't always control my situations, but I can control my decisions. Today I take control. I realize I have the power to change.

Day 14

Today I will tune up my attitude by making a commitment to never give up on anyone, since I know that miracles can happen every day. I know winners never quit, and quitters never win. First and foremost, I will never give up on myself.

Day 15

Today I will tune up my attitude by starting my new pattern of giving thanks every day and by saying "thank you" at least 15 times a day. My two most important "thank you's" will be when I wake up in the morning and just before I go to bed at night; thanking life itself.

Day 16

Today I will tune up my attitude by starting to live every facet of my life so that when others think of fairness, caring, and integrity, they think of me. If I am a parent, I will make sure that my children see these principles in action in our home at all times.

Day 17

Today I will tune up my attitude by creating the habit to do nice things for people who may never find out I've done them. It's not important for me to be recognized for doing something kind.

Day 18

Today I will tune up my attitude by planning a vacation—whether it is mental or physical—in my mind. I will use this day to recharge my attitude. I realize that taking time to relax my mind and body is important to my health, my happiness, and everyone I come in contact with.

Day 19

Today I will tune up my attitude by reading a book or listening to an audiotape on self-improvement. I will take the time, starting today, to invest in me. I accept my promotion to president of Me, Inc. I will commit to reading or listening daily to words that will enhance my growth. I will invest in the power of prayer.

Day 20

Today I will tune up my attitude by dreaming to be more than I was yesterday. Everything starts in my mind. I will take the pros and cons of yesterday and expand my vision, which I know will expand my actions and, in turn, improve my life.

Day 21

Today I will tune up my attitude by looking again at my chart to determine those areas of my life in which I still need to work. I will pledge to live my life according to the principles and practices expressed in this book.

> *Remember, by focusing on*
> *your attitude, you will always stay*
> *tuned up.*
>
> *—Keith D. Harrell*

*A*im to stay in focus.

*T*ake control of all your negative thoughts.

*T*ransform all challenges into opportunities.

*I*nspire someone with your faith today.

*T*eam up with other winning people.

*U*nderstand your own uniqueness.

*D*ream to be more than you are.

*E*xperience enthusiasm; it's essential for success.

If you make the effort and do all the things outlined in this book, life will still present its challenges. Adversities, tough times, and misfortunes are strangers to no one. Life is unpredictable: life is sometimes hard, and staying positive isn't always easy. It takes concentration, and it takes effort. Sometimes even when you make the effort, even if you are positive most of the time, it may not be enough. Life takes much more than just positive thinking; positive thinking *by itself* really didn't get me anything in my life. However, positive thinking, along with faith, hard work, and a good plan or strategy, enabled me to produce successful results.

When you compare positive thinking to negative thinking, you must understand that positive thinking will do more for your life than negative thinking any day of the week. Positive thinking gave me the faith to write this book; positive thinking motivated me to outline a plan on how I could write it, and positive thinking motivated me to finish it and update it.

I wish you the very best as you use your positive attitude, faith, hard work, and plan or strategy to enjoy the wonderful experience we call life. Don't ever forget: The choices you made yesterday have determined your success today. The choices you make today will determine your success tomorrow. Your attitude is a choice . . . *your* choice.

QUOTES FOR YOUR ATTITUDE

It's so hard when I have to, and so
easy when I want to.

—Sondra Anice Barnes

Even if you're on the right track,
you'll get run over if you just sit there.

—Will Rogers

I feel *super-fantastic*™!

—Keith D. Harrell

Recommended Reading List

for

Chapter 11

Live Your Dreams
by Les Brown

*Think and Grow Rich:
A Black Choice*
by Dennis Kimbro and Napoleon Hill

*You Can If You
Think You Can*
by Dr. Norman Vincent Peale

12

DEVELOPING YOUR SIX-MONTH ATTITUDE CHECK-UP PLAN

*Give everything in life
a positive attitude.*

—Keith D. Harrell

Congratulations!

You've made it through the book. You've completed the Attitude Discovery Chart on page 184. I hope you have already begun your 21-day Attitude Plan.

All of that is a great beginning. However, this is *just* a beginning. You will discover that your progress is better in some areas than others, and you will discover that—in a lot of areas—improvement has led to a desire for even greater improvement.

That's the purpose of this chapter—to help make your attitude tune-up what the people in business call a "continuous improvement program." In other words, you are going to get better and you are going to keep getting better.

The six-month check-up is simple—just four steps—and, because of the work you've already done, each of the four steps will be easier and more comfortable than what you have been doing thus far.

Step 1: Make an appointment with yourself for an attitude check-up.

Get out your calendar and pick a date approximately six months from now. WRITE IT DOWN. This is an important appointment, at least as important as the dental appointment you've already written down. (You should also keep this book where you can find it. You'll need it for your appointment.)

Don't Quit

When things go wrong, as they sometimes will,
When the road you're trudging seems all uphill,
When the funds are low, and the debts are high,
And you want to smile, but you have to sigh,
When care is pressing you down a bit,
Rest if you must, but don't you quit.
Life is queer with its twists and turns,
As every one of us sometimes learns,
And many a failure turns about,
When he might have won had he stuck it out.
Don't give up though the pace seems slow.
You may succeed with another blow.
Success is failure turned inside out,
The silver tint of the clouds of doubt,
And you never can tell how close you are,
It may be near when it seems so far,
So stick to the fight when you're hardest hit.
It's when things seem worse,
That you must not quit.

—Adopted from a poster I saw while
attending an IBM sales training class

Make that appointment right now:

My Six-Month Attitude Check-Up:

_____

Step 2: Fill out the Attitude Discovery Chart on page 203.

This one is just like the one in the last chapter with a single exception: add another column and label it "Positive, but could be more positive." You may find that in some areas your attitude is neutral or even negative, and in others, it's positive. In some, your attitude is positive, and you can really tell a difference. Now, you want to make an even greater difference.

Be honest with yourself. Thinking that "with all I'm going through, my attitude is about as positive as it can be" is letting circumstances dictate attitude. Remember, our attitude dictates our response to circumstances. If your attitude is negative or neutral in any area, check "negative" or "neutral." Be happy that you are going to do something about it.

Step 3: Analyze and evaluate the Attitude Discovery Chart.

Look at the areas in which you have shown an improvement. Congratulate yourself on making an important change in your life. You are no longer letting circumstances dictate your attitude; *you* are in charge.

Next, look at any areas you have checked as "negative" or "neutral." Discover why you consider this neutral or negative and think about what a more positive attitude will do for you. If you are counterproductive, refocus on your goals, review your plan of action, and think about the end result. Develop your own 21-day plan for improvement. Each day, tell yourself that you can make a difference and then use your plan to prove that.

Finally, look at the areas marked "Positive, but could be more positive." This is where you'll want to take another giant step in improving your attitude. Think about what "more" is and what it will do for you. Then make a 21-day plan, a very specific one, for reaching that goal.

Attitude Discovery Chart

	Neutral	Negative	Counter-Productive	Positive	Positive but could be more positive
Career or Education					
Family/ Personal Relationships					
Financial Situation					
Personal Development					
Physical Condition					
Social or Community Involvement					
Spiritual Life					

Step 4: Set up your follow-up appointment.

Pick out a date approximately six months away from your first check-up and make another appointment for yourself. When you feel the difference, you'll want to do this again.

ARE YOU FINISHED YET?

Maintaining a positive attitude is never truly completed. As long as we're breathing, we have the ability—the need—to learn and grow. We can all choose to change our attitude and, as you learned in this book, that takes action—daily action.

Adjusting our attitude is a day-by-day journey for all of us. It happens one action at a time. To keep the goal in front of me, I developed an acronym encompassing six key attitudes. These attitudes impact our performance at the personal and organizational level and create what I call S.P.I.R.I.T. I've used this acronym as the basis for workshops in numerous corporations. You might find the following synopsis from my new book helpful as a guide in your daily attitude tune-up.

S stands for **Self-awareness**

As we practiced the attitude tune-ups in this book, we became more aware of who we truly are—the values and beliefs that influence our attitude in action—and we consciously chose to make some changes. All change

begins with learning. Learning begins with self-awareness—a willing attitude to take an honest look at ourselves either as individuals or as an organization. The
ability to continue to learn and grow depends on our
commitment to examine our own behavior on a regular
basis and on our openness to the feedback of others.
Self-awareness gives us clues about what's really going
on inside and tells us "It's time for an attitude tune-up."
You will find yourself performing better—growing in
confidence and self-respect—and achieving new success
in all areas of your life.

P stands for **Purpose** and **Passion**

Life is only meaningful when you have a purpose and
the passion to pursue it. When our vision is right, passion and its derivatives—commitment, perseverance, and
persistence—follow naturally. Personal leadership is the
key—the ability to keep a positive attitude in the pursuit of our plan even when it does not go smoothly. As
you continue to listen to your inner voice, you fine tune
your purpose and recognize "true" opportunities. You
find your enthusiasm growing as you experience the joy
of self-fulfillment.

I stands for **Initiative**

How do we respond to our daily challenges? How do
we react to change? How do we perform under stress?
The answer lies in our attitude of initiative. Initiative
means that we proactively meet challenges, embrace

change, learn continuously, and take risks to achieve our goals. You become a peak performer—personally and professionally—as you take control of circumstances rather than letting external factors dictate the direction of your day.

R stands for **Relationships** and **Respect**

If we approach every interaction with others with an attitude of respect and consideration, the quality of our personal and professional relationships will transform. Respect opens the door for effective communication because it allows us to lay aside judgment, to listen attentively, to operate from a spirit of cooperation, and to value the unique contributions of others. You experience deeper understanding and harmony in your relationships.

I stands for **Insight**

Insight—the ability to discern the true meaning of a situation—is important to making good decisions individually or as part of a work team. It requires an open mind and an open heart—looking at the bigger picture, seeing opportunities beyond the obvious, and valuing the ideas and opinions of others. Expanding your mental horizon gives insights that lead to innovative solutions that benefit all.

T stands for **Trust**

Trust is an important attitude for uniting the efforts of any group who works together with a shared vision toward common goals. When we trust others and others trust us, we let go of our own agenda to seek solutions for the common good. Trust enables us to share ownership of an idea, to lead or to serve, to value opinions different from our own, and to consider options that stretch our comfort zone. It provides you with the environment for family unity, community cooperation, and work team effectiveness.

Remember, your attitude is your most priceless possession. I wish you a *super-fantastic*™ journey in discovering the power that lies within you—Attitude Is Everything!

——————————

For information on Keith Harrell's products or services please visit our web site at www.Super-Fantastic.com or call (800) 451-3190.